ARTISAN
PUBLIC RELATIONS

ARTISAN PUBLIC RELATIONS

PAUL WAGNER

WINE APPRECIATION GUILD
SAN FRANCISCO

Wine Appreciation Guild
an imprint of
Board and Bench Publishing
www.boardandbench.com
Edited by Margaret Clark
Design and composition by Chris Matulich
Library of Congress Cataloging-in-publication is on file with the Library of Congress

Printed in the United States of America

CONTENTS

Acknowledgments

Artisan Food and Beverage Producers

This book is a work that has been thirty-five years in the making. That's how long I have been working in the world of food and wine. I have represented cheese companies, water companies, juice drinks, wine, beer, olive oil, coffees, teas, restaurants, and a seemingly endless list of other artisan products. I may not have made millions, but I certainly have eaten and drunk like a king. And I have my clients to thank for that, God bless them.

I should also thank the many bright and willing employees who have worked at Balzac over the years. They have brought energy, expertise, and creativity to my world, and I hope that I have given them something in return. I know that some of them will recognize their work in the pages that follow.

Equally important, I need to thank the hundreds of students at Napa Valley College who have taken my courses and challenged me to think in new ways about the same old problems. I love the fact that they ask me the hard questions, and don't always accept my glib answers.

Some of this book began as a series of articles in *Vineyard and Winery Management*, where I wrote a column for more than ten years for the wine business, with a focus on smaller producers who couldn't afford a large agency. Publisher Rob Merletti has kindly given me permission to reprint some of that material, and I've been delighted to see how well it was suited to this new purpose.

I should thank Bryan Imelli of Board and Bench Publishing, who suggested that this book might be a good idea. I think he was right. We'll see.

And finally, my beloved wife, Margaret, who continues to endure the endless work of making what I write make sense. After forty-two years, she still hasn't given up.

INTRODUCTION

SUCCESSFUL STRATEGIES AND TACTICS FOR SMALL PRODUCERS OF WINE, BEER, BREAD, OLIVE OIL AND CHEESE*

When I first started working in public relations, a generation ago, there was a classic description of the perfect public relations director. She would be cute, blond, and perky. Her career often started out in the retail store, tasting room, or as a personal assistant, and then grew to include local tastings, major festivals, and the organization of company events. And that was the job.

Well, I am not cute, I am not blond, and I am very rarely perky, but after many years of working in public relations for small wineries,

---

* This book is based loosely on more than ten years of articles I wrote as a columnist for one of the leading trade magazines in the wine industry, *Vineyard and Winery Management*. And so while a majority of the examples in this book naturally refer to wine, the strategies, tactics and execution apply to any business that is putting its heart and soul into the artisan production of something good to eat or drink. After all, during that time, our agency represented some of the most interesting clients in wine, as well as artisan producers of cheese, olive oil, crackers, beer, bottled water...etc. And yes, we really enjoyed sampling the products!

breweries and olive oil companies and cheesemakers, I think I know what it takes to be successful.

It turns out that being blond is not really that important.

Over the past twenty-five years, food and wine-related brand marketing programs have evolved from a few shelf-talkers and table tents to huge sponsorships of everything from the Academy Awards and NASCAR to breast cancer research and public television.

And public relations campaigns have gone from private invitations to a few key writers to massive national campaigns. It used to be that a nice press kit and a smiling face could usually get you some coverage. Now we see celebrity chefs, podcasts, and concert tour logistics have all become part of the package.

While individual producers are often still small, artisan food and beverages have become big business, and public relations programs have grown up alongside the industry.

But for most smaller producers, the challenges still remain—as they do for all small businesses. They don't have the dollars to compete on a national scale, and their only hope for success in the world of public relations is to be more cost-effective, more targeted, and smarter than their competition.

Cute, blond, and perky? Nope. Try smart, effective, and focused.

Making sure that's how you approach your public relations effort is what this book is all about.

CHAPTER 1

WHAT IS PUBLIC RELATIONS?

When hand-crafted artisan producers or other small companies think about Public Relations, they usually have a very simple, straightforward goal: They want to see front-page stories about themselves in the local or national press, or in the top trade journals. What they don't understand is that such stories are not written on the spur of the moment, nor are they written as the result of some cleverly worded pitch by a creative Public Relations expert. They are usually written because they capture the news of the moment in a way that is clear and memorable.

But there is far more to Public Relations than just a news story. There are myriad ways that a small company can use the strategies and tactics of Public Relations to help them achieve their marketing goals, and build a very successful business. Some of them are astonishingly easy, and others take years to develop and execute. Some are expensive, and others cost little more than the time it takes to make a phone call. And some require a full-time Public Relations professional, while others can be done by just about anyone in the privacy of their own home.

How do you know which ones are for you? That's what this book is all about.

You may have noticed that I have already made a couple of assumptions. In the second paragraph above, I assumed that you are trying to achieve your marketing goals, and build a successful business. That means you need a clear understanding of how your business will be successful, and you need a set of clear marketing goals that have been defined to help you achieve that success.

If you don't have those, you can't do good PR. You can flop around and make a lot of noise, but it won't get you what you want.

What's the solution?

You NEED a business plan. I was asked a few years ago to work on a project for the Italian Ministry of Agriculture to develop a basic marketing communications plan for small family wineries in Italy. These wineries were suffering in the face of larger national and international competition, and the ministry wanted to provide some kind of a plan to help them fight back.

I was honored and delighted. I immediately asked them to send me a copy of the business plan they had developed, so that I could create a marketing plan that would be successful.

My contact in Italy was astonished. "But they don't have a business plan!" he cried. "They are family businesses!"

Exactly. And without a business plan, they don't know how they can make more money.

So before you get excited about all of the things in this book, please develop a very basic business plan for your company. It should explain how much it costs to make each product, and what your expenses are for keeping the doors open. And it should give you a very clear idea of how many customers you need, and how much each customer needs to buy. If you don't know those facts, then you can't really plan how to improve your marketing.

It's a simple equation. If you know how much you have to sell, and you know what your average sale is, then you know how many customers you'll need to meet those goals. Those basic figures will give you, and everyone else on your team, the information they need to be successful.

You should start by making sure that everyone on the team understands your business plan. The only way you can be sure that your Public Relations team is really focused on the best possible programs for you is to give them the information they need to succeed. If you really want them to do the best possible job for you, they need to know how you are going to make the best return on your investment.

Examples of the importance of this communication abound. Because Public Relations professionals are trained to respond aggressively to any indication of interest by the media, they sometimes find themselves selling stories that have no long term benefit for the brand, and may even distract the winery's key audiences from more important messages.

I once consulted for a hospital whose marketing director was horrified to learn that three departments of the hospital were producing newsletters and other marketing materials to encourage patients to partake of their services. He was horrified because the departments in question lost money for the hospital every time they treated a patient. Because the management of the hospital had never communicated the overall business plan to the employees, a significant portion of the marketing budget was being spent on loss leaders, with no real benefits to the hospital.

Do you think this doesn't happen in the rest of the world?

Inexperienced companies often chase media attention simply because they see the opportunity for coverage, despite the fact that the coverage may not be in the best long-term interest on the company. If the business plan for the company calls for a focus on the most profitable products, then the Public Relations efforts should fully reflect this focus.

Some companies have specifically increased the production of product lines that generate almost nothing for the bottom line, only because the media response to them is so positive. Years later, when sales of the more profitable lines in the portfolio have decreased, and the company finds itself making vast amounts of low-priced, unprofitable products, the error becomes obvious. By then, it is a much harder problem to solve. In fact, the company has apparently worked hard to earn a well-established reputation for making products that will not survive the next big economic slump. And it's particularly easy for smaller, artisan producers to focus on making products that don't make money, because, after all, this is a labor of love. Sadly, that's not a sustainable business plan.

Public Relations is not something that can be successful on a spontaneous basis. It requires careful strategic planning and exceptional professional execution. And the very first thing it requires is a clear vision of the goals of the business—a map for success.

What is Public Relations? I'll give you a more extensive definition in future chapters, but for the purposes of this chapter, let's just define it as relationships with the various publics of your company. And what's the goal of Public Relations? It's to manage the perceptions of those publics.

What perceptions do we want them to have? That's a question for the marketing department. Which means that Public Relations is a function of marketing. If you don't have a clear marketing plan, complete with a fully developed brand statement and positioning, then your public relations efforts will not be accurately targeted.

Only a clear understanding of the business plan will give the Public Relations and Marketing teams the information they need to create a successful strategy. Remember what the Cheshire Cat advised Alice in Wonderland:

> *"Would you tell me, please, which way I ought to go from here?" asked Alice.*
> *"That depends a good deal on where you want to get to," said the cat.*
> *"I don't much care where," said Alice.*
> *"Then it doesn't matter which way you go," said the cat.*
> —*Lewis Carroll, Alice's Adventures in Wonderland*

Why don't more companies share this critical information with their employees?

Fear

If you as the owner or manager are afraid to explain your business plan to the employees, often it is because you don't want to provide the employees with the information they need to judge the effectiveness of the management. After all, if the employees don't know what the overall business goals are, then they can't very well question the judgment of the management in reaching these goals.

The underlying message here is clear: that the company management and its employees are somehow not on the same team, do not have good communications skills, and are working at cross-purposes. If this is the case, then the solution is to solve those root problems, not keep the employees in the dark.

Often, this fear has an even more obvious source: the management or owners of the company would like to obscure the profitability from the employees. As a business owner, I recognize this as a key management issue, but one that must be addressed. If the employees do not share in the vision for the future, and do not share in the ultimate goals of the business, then they are working at a disadvantage. Their efforts will be hampered by this lack of knowledge, and the results they achieve will be distorted by their ignorance.

Mistrust

Some companies are sure that providing sensitive information to their employees is asking for trouble. Again, this is misidentifying the problem. If you have hired employees that you cannot trust, then you must address that issue. If you CAN trust your employees, then you must give them the information they need to successfully perform their jobs for you.

I once had the enviable position of visiting a series of companies that all competed very directly with each other. Each one assured me that what I saw at their company was truly unique, and their production processes were proprietary secrets that gave them a competitive edge in the marketplace. After visiting all of the companies, I was amused to realize that virtually every one of the companies used an identical process. There was no proprietary information. And yet the companies were all extremely concerned about secrecy and discretion.

I don't think very many people believe that there are real trade secrets in the wine industry. Production methods are shared throughout the world. Marketing information and analysis are readily available for anyone who has a checkbook and a computer. And yet companies often have a hard time being completely open and honest with their employees about their business plans.

Sloth

Finally, there is the question of time. Nobody has enough of it, and time spent talking to the employees is time that could be spent talking to customers or suppliers. It is ironic that in our world of artisan foods and beverages we frequently complain that restaurants are unwilling to invest the time it takes to train their servers in our products, yet we do not spend more time training our own employees in our vision and goals.

How many artisan companies have regular quarterly meetings of the staff so that they can review progress, understand the key issues facing the company, and plan for better results in the next six months? How many employees could give a focused tour of the facility, covering all the key messages in the marketing plan? For that matter, how many companies make sure that their own employees know about any special marketing programs for the current quarter? How many companies copy their employees on press releases? I am always amazed that the staff of tasting rooms never seem to know what the marketing department is doing to help sell the products on a national basis, and yet are asked to entertain the same customers, provide them with information, and hope that their efforts are on target and on message.

It's a Question of Priorities

I have spoken at a lot of conferences over the years. I love meeting the many owners and employees who attend these conferences, and I enjoy the give-and-take conversations that take place at them.

But one thing has always amused me about these conferences. They generally have two seminar tracks: one for the technical side of the business, and one for marketing and sales. For most artisan producers, that means that one person (the beer/cheese/winemaker) attends the production track, and the other person (the sales/marketing/PR person) attends the marketing track, where I am speaking.

The seminars are always fun and educational, but I always find myself thinking, "The wrong people are in this seminar. The people who really need to hear this presentation are next door, learning about all the various technical aspects of making the product." So many artisan companies begin as a hobby. But unless they are tied directly to a business plan that includes developing a successful marketing and sales plan, these artisans will never make the leap into a sustainable business.

Success isn't just about making good products. My grandmother made great food. But she never became a business. Forget that old saying that if you build a better mousetrap, people will beat a path to your door. First of all, nobody is looking for a better mousetrap. And secondly, the artisan food industry creates subjective products where terms like "better" and "best" are rarely used with much effect. For more on this, see Chapter Sixteen.

Want an even better argument against focusing all your efforts on production? In the wine business, the *Wine Spectator* plays a big role in helping unknown wineries leap into the spotlight. But these days, the *Wine Spectator* "gives" those highly sought-after scores of 90 points and higher to roughly 6,500 wines. So making a wine that gets 92 points isn't going to make you stand out from the crowd—its going to put you smack dab in a crowd that has 7,000 other wines in it. Making good wine is not enough.

Making good products is NOT the solution to your marketing and communications problems; it's the basic entry fee to be in business at all. If you are not making good products, you should close your doors. But don't make the mistake of thinking that making good products will solve all your problems. Even a nice review for one of your products really only gets you a shiny new uniform. It doesn't get you on the field where you can really play the game. That's where PR and marketing come in.

So what does success mean for artisan producers of foods or beverages? Success isn't making good products. Success is making a product and selling it at a good profit. And that means that you should spend as much time thinking about how you are going to sell your product at a profit as you do thinking about how you make it.

What's the solution? Time, focus, and energy. It's that simple. Yes, I know that your goats or your sheep are demanding of your time and energy, every day. Batches of beer must be coddled along. Grapevines must be pruned, trellised, fed and watered. So how many bottles of wine does a grapevine produce? Let's just say for sheer fun that your grapevines produce about three to four bottles of wine each per year.

By happy coincidence, this is also about the number of bottles each one of your customers will buy each year.

Do you see where I am going with this? Why is it that artisan producers of great products think that their production process should get attention eight or ten or 365 times per year, but the customer only gets attention when they walk in the door?

Step One of the solution is to make sure that every time someone goes out into your vineyard or your brewery or to tend your cows, someone else should spend the same amount of time contacting each one of your customers and talking to them about your products. Yes, that is a lot of time. It is also time well-spent achieving the goals of your business. Your customers are absolutely as critical to your success as anything you do in the production department. And you need to believe that, and embrace it.

Step Two is to focus on learning as much about marketing and communication as you do about artisan production methods. My suggestion? Every time you spend an hour researching hops or barley, root stocks or yeasts, rennet or olive varieties, someone should be spending the same amount of time researching the best ways to communicate with your target audiences, or how to do marketing via public relations instead of advertising. Marketing and communications are highly valued skills, and should be learned and respected. You should focus on them just as intently.

Step Three? Give your public relations and marketing efforts the same kind of energy that you give to making your products. If you were to develop a new customer offer every time you racked your barrels, you would not only sell more wine; you would also have a much better relationship with your wine club members. That's a good thing, because your customers are much more likely to buy your cheese than your sheep are!

There you have it. Three simple steps to making your company more successful and more sustainable. Take the time, give them your focus, and invest the energy into them, and you will have a significant impact on your business outlook. Admittedly, it will take a lot of work to make them happen, but at least you will be doing work, and not exploring a hobby.

And may I add one more element to this tirade? At most artisan companies, the production team or owner decides what to make each year, based on what he or she is interested in producing. After all, this is how hobbies work. People engage in hobbies because they have fun, and they can do whatever they want. Real businesses base these important decisions on what their customers want to buy. Which means it shouldn't be the production team making these decisions at all.

It should be your marketing and sales team, based on what they have learned about their customers. Those same customers your sales team is talking to every time the production team is lost for days in the back room, experimenting, testing, tasting, and thinking that what they are doing is the most important part of the business.

Public Relations Defined

I like to define Public Relations as managing the relationships with your various publics. Yes, in terms of a definition it's just a little facile, but it also captures something that many public relations practitioners forget: There are many, many publics, and all are important. One of the most important audiences is the employees of the company itself. We'll talk more about this in the chapters to come.

But the point of this chapter is that if your own employees don't know the key marketing messages or believe them, you will not achieve success. The employees won't have the information they need for the daily decisions they make in their jobs—decisions that will, in the end, determine whether or not your company can deliver on the promise you and your marketing team are making to the world.

That's why you need to understand your business plan, and you need to explain it to your employees.

CHAPTER 2

WHAT'S MARKETING?

There are lots of definitions of marketing, from classic consumer product marketing (find a need in the market, and then fill it) to larger scale visions (develop and enhance the image of a brand.) One I particularly like is that marketing is defining everything a company does in terms of its customers.

The basis of all Marketing Communications is a simple construct: delivering a focused message to a targeted audience. There are three parts of this, and they are listed in reverse order, in my opinion. Because first you have to define your audience: who are they, what do they do, where do they live, and why should they be interested in your product? Then define the message: what are you, what are you selling, and why should that target audience care? Finally, we'll get to talk about delivering the message. But that's the next chapter.

Your Audience

Public Relations is building relationships with all of your various publics: owners, management, employees, distribution network, consumers, neighbors, local regulatory authorities, local and regional politicians, and yes, the media. Those who forget all the other audiences in their efforts to focus only on the media will ultimately pay the price.

Of course, for some of these audiences keeping their attention is an easy problem to solve. The owners stay awake at night thinking about

11

the company. The management is paid to think about the company, and the employees will always care about it, if only to protect their own livelihood. All that is required is that you keep them informed. And as we saw in the last chapter, that isn't always done effectively.

But the harder audiences are those for whom the competition is tougher. In a market saturated with thousands of brands and many thousands of choices, why should anyone care about yours?

Or as my mother used to say, What makes you think you're so special?

That, more than any other single question, is the crux to doing good public relations at any level. If you can't answer it in fewer than seven words, you will always have a problem in the market.

Why seven words? We all know the story of "Snow White and the Seven Dwarfs." We have seen the film many times, both as children and with our own children. We have heard the story or read the book many more times. This is a part of our lives from early childhood onwards. And yet hardly anyone can list the names of all seven dwarfs. It's true. I give this as a quiz in my marketing communications classes at Napa Valley College, and fewer than 5% of the students can list all seven.* Why? The ratio of numbers of names to the importance of the information is too high.

If you would argue that the limit should be ten words, ask any group of people to list the Ten Commandments. You will find the same results— even among devout Catholics.

In today's saturated market, you have to work hard, and edit fiercely, to come up with a message that is really memorable. If you can't remember the seven dwarfs, you cannot expect a distributor, writer, or retailer to remember a long list of key elements of your story.

If you have ever made a distributor presentation, you know how challenging they are. You are one of twelve companies at a trade show, given fifteen minutes each to tell your story. Only one or two of those companies will have the kind of simple, direct, and easy-to-understand message that the salespeople will remember. The rest will be forgotten, blurred in a fog of products, brands, personalities, and promises that will disappear from memory within twenty-four hours.

---

* The "Y" dwarves are usually easiest: Happy, Grumpy, Sneezy, Dopey, and Sleepy. The others, Doc and Bashful, are always harder to remember.

And consumers? While you may be convinced that consumers love your products, and know all about them, I would encourage you to do a little hardball market research. Dig just a little underneath that initial impression, and you will find that consumers know almost nothing about your company or brand. And what they think they know is often incorrect.

Is There Any There, There?

The single most challenging part of creating a good public relations program is usually far outside the realm of the public relations department. If the company or brand isn't founded on a unique proposition, then the public relations campaign is already handcuffed, long before any events are held, articles are written, or samples are sent.

In many ways, the media works much like your distribution network. The only reason they want to buy your product is so that they can re-sell it at a profit. For the media this means you have to provide the kind of interesting story that their readers really want to read. It's not enough that you think it is interesting, or that your mother would want to read it. The story has to be good enough to get people who know nothing about you to dive into it and read it from beginning to end.

Is Your Story Good Enough? For Most Small Companies, The Answer Is No

Almost all artisan producers do a comparative tasting of products, to make sure that the price and quality of their products are realistically positioned within the category. (From a statistical basis, these tastings are often completely inaccurate and misleading, but that's another topic entirely.) The results are used to help the marketing department refine its pricing strategies, and help the production team refine its approach.

But how many small companies perform this same analysis on their basic marketing messages? How many artisan food producers can tell you exactly how their marketing and messaging compares to that of the competition? Very few. And even fewer take the results of these studies and use them to create the kind of story that both media and the market will find compelling.

The goal of any marketing campaign must be to take a leadership position in a category. This is the most basic marketing precept, memorized by every first year marketing student. It should be engraved on the lintel over every marketing office in our industry. Because this is where our marketing communication falls down hard. Most producers cannot define the category in which they compete. They cannot explain how they are going to achieve this most basic goal of becoming the category leader.

And with the explosion of artisan cheeses, craft beers, boutique olive oil mills, and wineries in all fifty states, it's only going to get more difficult. There aren't going to be a lot of leaders. There are going to be a lot of followers. In fact, most of these companies won't play the game to win; they will play the game just to be on the field. This may be fun for the owners for a while, but when it comes to telling a compelling story to the media, this leaves a public relations program in a very difficult situation.

To continue the sports analogy, very few mediocre players get national attention. And yet companies that don't play to win always seem to want the media to write big stories about them. It isn't going to happen.

How Does This Play Out in the Day-to-Day World of Public Relations?

The first thing you should do is to define yourself in as few words as possible. The goal is simple. The marketing message must be short—fewer than seven words. It must be in language that really reaches the people in the marketplace—because it will have to convince their hearts, not just inform their minds. And it must be unique—and that is the really hard one.

The more you try to satisfy those three criteria, the more you will realize that the only solution is to play the game to win. It is not enough to be one of the better cheese companies in your town. Readers want to read about the best one, not one of the better ones. It's not enough to be more or less organic with most of your oils. Readers want to know about the people who are really trying the hardest, not those who are making a half-hearted effort.

Nor is it enough to say something outlandishly powerful and definitive about yourself. Because for obvious reasons, it must also be true.

When I call the media about a story, I always want to be able to answer a couple of very basic questions.

1. Is this true? If you have provided the media with misleading or erroneous information, then your story will not get written. Even worse, it might get written, only to be corrected at a later date. Either way, you will have lost all credibility with the writer and the readers, and neither you nor your company will ever get serious consideration again.

2. Are you the best example of this position? If not, then you can expect the media to know about the others, and to write about the others, not you. Once again, you will lose credibility for suggesting that you are the leader, when you are simply a follower.

3. Does this story have to be written today? If not, then you can expect the writer to put it on the back burner, and write about more timely stories today. When will your story get resuscitated? When the writer has lots of time, or runs out of any other timely stories to write. Neither is good news.

Marketing classes teach us to perform a SWOT analysis on our products, to make sure that we are developing a clean and clear message about the company and its products. Identifying the Strengths, Weaknesses, Opportunities and Threats is a key element to the creation of any marketing plan—or even starting a business. But artisan producers often neglect this process, because they are driven by passion rather than good common sense. That works for a while, as they get into the business as a hobby. But that's not enough if you want to own a real, sustainable business. You need to be able to tell everyone what you do better than anyone else—those are your strengths. And you need to recognize what you don't do well, and how both of those factors will play out in the foreseeable future for your business.

Artisan producers rarely start this way. They usually find themselves fighting these battles five, ten or more years on, as they finally realize that they are in a competitive market, and they need a plan. That's a pity, because such an analysis could give direction to any number of companies that are currently struggling in the marketplace. Here's a simple outline for how to approach it.

A SWOT analysis simply asks you to list the Strengths, Weaknesses, Opportunities and Threats for your company. It is an excellent outline of exactly the kinds of questions that any good writer will ask you—and any good distributor as well.

What do you do best? Do you do it better than anyone else? Why? Why not? What are your weaknesses? Why don't you fix them? Why don't you eliminate products that are not the best of their type? After working though each one of these questions, and coming up with the brutally honest answers for each one, you will be confronted with the ultimate question—the question that is keeping you from achieving the kind of success you would like in Public Relations:

What would you have to change in your business to make a difference? What do you have to do to be one of the artisan producers that really wins, rather than just plays the game?

Suddenly, Public Relations doesn't seem to be about pretty pictures, pleasant events, and friendly people. Public Relations now appears in its true form: a basic structuring of the business so that it lives and breathes a compelling story.

How Good Does the Story Have to Be?

You already know that answer to that question. If you are playing to win, the story has to be better than anyone else's. In the same way that your products should win more awards and get better reviews, your story has to be the best one in the category—the most compelling one in the market.

One evening at Napa Valley College, Amelia Ceja came to me after class and asked me to help her with the Public Relations campaigns for Ceja winery. I had known the family for years, and was immediately pre-disposed to help. But as she told me the story of her family and how they worked themselves up from below the ground floor to achieve the American Dream, I knew that I wouldn't help them.

It wasn't that they had problems I couldn't solve. In fact, their story was so perfect, their wines were so good, that I knew they didn't need my help. And I told her so. I gave her the names of a few media to contact, I made a couple of contacts myself, and the winery has been featured throughout the country in everything from major wine magazines to newspapers, lifestyle, and even television. They didn't need help, they just needed to get started.

Is your story as good as theirs? If not, it's time to start thinking beyond a press release, a media luncheon, or a sample mailing. It's time to start thinking about the essence of your message, and how you can make it more interesting. It's time to play the game to win.

If you are going to do that, you need a game plan. So with the above in mind, let's lay out how to develop a marketing communications game plan.

If you think of public relations in its simplest form, you often think of working with the media to get your message out to your various audiences or publics. And if there is one thing that we can guarantee about the media as a whole, it is that it is unpredictable at best. While there are any number of "regular" stories in the media, from Veterans' Day to New Year's Eve, the biggest stories of the year are always a surprise. After all, that's why they call it the news!

(Of course, I have suggested that Public Relations goes far beyond working with just the media, but the long term goal is still the same. And the unpredictability is also the same.)

That doesn't mean you shouldn't have a plan. We love clients who work with us to develop a long range plan for the year. That plan gives us everything we need to do good work for the client for the next twelve months, and both we and the client have agreed on what we are going to try to achieve. That makes the work a lot more rewarding.

For some of our clients, such as the major wine regions in Europe, this kind of a plan is a critical part of the funding process. Without such a plan, they cannot get funding from their members or support from government programs. In other words, they want to know what they are going to get, and they want that information to be as specific as possible. Since we've worked with some of these groups for many, many years, we're very comfortable with the process and the terminology. It's a great way to have everyone on the same page from the beginning. But there are drawbacks to the European system, and we'll get into those later in this chapter.

So what goes into a good year-long public relations plan? We start with the basics:

Positioning and key messages: If you don't have these, you simply can't do good marketing or Public Relations. You need to define who you are in terms of your competition, and you need to do it in a way that is easy for your customers to understand and repeat. If you don't know your messaging, there is no reason to contact anyone else. You have nothing to say. A good public relations plan will have this messaging right at the top. That will help you work with graphic designers as well—since they need this information to capture your messaging in graphics.

Audiences and key markets: You cannot be all things to all people. You have to refine your plan so that it focuses on those markets that are most important to you. As an artisan producer, you should already know that you are selling to a smaller portion of the overall U.S. market, so that's a start. By definition, your products aren't for everyone. Now it's time to get more specific about that. A good game plan will identify those markets that need extra support to grow, as well as those markets that are so important that they must get attention to keep the sales flowing. And your audience goals should also clarify the roles that restaurants and retailers play in your business. Smaller producers will want a tight geographic focus, so that they don't waste money trying to reach people who are not in a position to become customers. For every audience, you should have messaging and a plan, and you should have a list of audiences for your plan. Don't forget your own employees, local authorities and regulatory agencies, and the people who can make your life miserable...like your neighbors!

Expected developments: a calendar of events. Every company has a projection for sales activities that includes new releases, new label introductions, and the like. These projections form the building blocks of an annual plan. You need to send your products out to the media when they are first released, not when they have been in market for ten months. That's not news. So your public relations plan should include all of these dates, with supporting activities. This is also where you need to list any plans for future expansion into new markets, and how you are going to support those with Public Relations efforts, as well as any key events in which you participate.

Once you have all of these basics in line, you can start to work on the delivery systems. You will want to map out when you will use press releases or media pitches to get the key messages to those audiences. The new label story should be sent to your entire distribution network, along with any marketing materials you have developed to support it. New products need new fact sheets updated on the website. All of this can be charted out well in advance, so that you should never find yourself selling into the marketplace without the appropriate support materials.

If you sell outside your local area, you need to include a section of the plan that addresses when your top management will travel to those markets to support the brand. Try to plan this out in advance to the point of identifying key writers you may want to meet during the visit. Major writers often book their schedules months in advance, so it is important to check these dates with the writers and make sure that they are open. You should also be able to identify special events that you have selected to reach particular groups or audiences. In future chapters I'll write about how important these events are—and how important it is to have measurable goals and objectives for them. Write it all out as part of your plan, so that you can always know (and SHOW!) how you are doing.

If you have the money to organize your own events at the company or in other locations, these should also be included in the public relations plan and calendar. Everybody needs friends. Sure, you have a few, but you can always use more, can't you? Part of making friends is finding strategic alliances with partners who share your goals and interests, but don't compete for your customers. It is not always possible to lay out the complete strategic alliance at the beginning of the year, but you should have a few options in the plan. And if you have some of these in place, then you must have a clear idea of what you expect them to do for you. Write it out and track it.

Here is a key element to building a plan: you need to have measurable objectives that you hope to achieve. As an example, we once developed a very targeted approach for a major client. We identified the key publications that really influenced sales in their industry, and then we pitched specific stories, focusing on their key company messages, to the writers who wrote those stories. Those are measurable goals. Add in goals for every other public that you have on your list of audiences, and now you have a scorecard to keep track of how you are doing. We'll talk about this in more detail in Chapter Fifteen when we get into the nitty gritty of planning and evaluation.

I'd only suggest that having a plan and goals is a really good idea. So is paying attention to how you are doing, so that you can adjust the plan to be more successful. It's great that you are really focused on specific strategies, but remember that if they don't work, even if you love them, it's time to change something. That's all part of a good marketing and PR strategy. After all, marketing is like warfare, and good generals know that you have to be willing to adjust your plans to conditions and resources.

What's Your Story?

I once had a fascinating conversation with José Peñín, the leading wine writer in Spain. His Peñín Guide to Spanish wine is a massive one-thousand-page tome that reviews more than nine thousand brands with tasting notes, comments on the wineries, and thoughtful insights into the future of Spanish wine and food. It is the Bible for Spanish wine.

As you might imagine, many wineries in Spain turn to Mr. Peñín not just for tasting notes, but also advice on what they need to do to be successful. We spent a few very enjoyable minutes talking about the state of wine marketing in the world today, and I was delighted to learn that his answers very much mirror my own thoughts.

He explained that far too many wineries think that the solution to success in the wine business is making good wine. In the current Peñín Guide he has a special section at the end of the book that lists the top wines from every region—a listing that includes more than two thousand wines. How can you expect to stand out from the crowd, when you are one of more than two thousand of the very best? You can't.

Make no mistake. These wines are really good. They just don't stand out, because there are so many really good wines on the market today: two thousand in Spain alone!

This situation is similar to the huge number of artisan food and beverage producers popping up in the U.S. these days.

Mr. Peñín's solution was simple. If most wines are well-made these days, then the winery must do something different to stand out—and by "different," he didn't mean using a slightly different toast on your oak barrel. He is fascinated by wineries that are exploring new (or very old!) and different regions, techniques and philosophies. "I can drink a 90+ point wine every day, if I choose," he said. "But I would prefer to drink a wine that is interesting, that has a story. It doesn't matter about the points. A story always adds flavor and character to a wine."

José also likes to say that he is sick and tired of seeing tanks and barrels every time he visits a winery. He claims to learn a lot more about the winemaker by meeting the winemaker's dog than by seeing those rows and rows of metal tanks.

I think you can see why he and I hit it off so well!

Four Keys:

Make good wine. You need to be on the field.
Know what makes you different.
Understand how your wine promises a destination.
Tell us why we should visit.

P.S.: And if you have a wine or winery with a great STORY, please let me know. José Peñín visits the U.S. from time to time, and he always asks me to find some interesting wineries for him to visit. He is interested in wines that are being made in a very new or very old way—whether that involves high tech solutions or ancient traditions. I can hardly wait to chat with him again!

CHAPTER 3

WHAT'S PR AGAIN?

It's simple. Public Relations is Relationships with publics. One of the secrets to any successful PR campaign is to make sure that all of your publics get the attention, messaging, and love they deserve.

Making artisan food and beverage products is the easy part. It's selling them that's hard! Then again, there are about two hundred thirty million adults in the USA. How many of those do you need to sell a few containers of artisan cheese or cases of wine?

So who are your publics? The best way to move ahead is make a list of them. While you are at it, take the time to identify what you want to communicate to each one. And then we can develop the delivery system in some of the later chapters.

Of course, when we are talking about artisan foods, one of the biggest challenges we have is that many people in the United States don't really understand or appreciate what we do. In fact, for most of us in the high end of the business, we are focusing most of our efforts on a very small percentage of the population that cares enough about really good food to track it down and pay for it. In some parts of the country more than fifty percent of the population doesn't drink alcoholic beverages at all, let alone wine. That's what is known as a difficult territory.

We are forced to focus our efforts on that small percentage of people who care about artisan products. And our budgets force us to be cost-effective. If you want to show results, you really have to make sure that you are fishing where the fish are, even if it means a very tough competition with all the other fishermen in the business.

It is possible to explore new territory, to fish where no fishermen have ever gone before—but it is very hard, and once you reach out beyond this select group of artisan food lovers to market a brand or wine to the larger public, it is usually not very cost-effective. Over the long term, as budgets get reviewed and management tightens the purse strings, these programs get the budgetary axe.

Our challenge is even more daunting when we look at what is needed to compete for the attention of the general interest media. Remember, our job is to provide the media with the kinds of stories and information that they can re-sell to their audiences. In the case of the general interest media, our competition is not only other artisan producers, but also includes two other groups that usually have the inside edge.

Obviously, since a large percentage of the population doesn't think that our products are a top priority, one of our biggest challenges is to create stories that will compete successfully against stories from industries of much broader public appeal. It would be lovely to think that the release of your new blue cheese is a major new story, but compared to the public's interest in the next release from Beyoncé or the Kardashians, your story suffers considerably in comparison.

Equally challenging is the need to compete against industries with far greater economic clout. The profit margins in our business will never give us the kinds of budgets that are available to the big corporate producers of distilled beverages, soft drinks, or sports drinks. And because we don't have the same kinds of budgets, we cannot put together the same kinds of programs.

In many cases, we in wine PR are encouraged to "THINK BIG"—to come up with that single great idea that will achieve massive amounts of consumer media attention. But we are rarely given the kinds of budgets that will allow us to compete for the attention of that media. Frankly, that's a good thing. A few small companies have spent significant portions of their budgets on these kinds of activities, but over the long run, the results have simply not panned out.

Why? Because our industry is different.

There is a strong element of distrust in many educated consumers. Particularly at the upper end of the price spectrum, we often see resistance to any overt marketing efforts. The clearly stated sentiment is that if an artisan producer has to resort to clever marketing schemes and promotions to sell their products, then there must be something wrong with the quality of the products themselves. This is best captured by the wonderful adage that "any artisan that can afford to advertise is too big to make really good stuff."

Clearly, this is inaccurate. Just as clearly, many consumers hold it to be true. In the world of marketing, perception is reality.

As public relations professionals, we are asked to give the general media a try. We are encouraged to place a certain amount of our effort against a major news opportunity, much in the way a gambler might place a small bet on a long shot, just in case he gets lucky. What most of our clients do not understand is that even if that long shot comes through, it will probably not have the impact on sales that they hope. Even when you are successful at major media placement, you may find that those who are seeing the results are not paying attention, and are not motivated to respond to your product.

In the end, we have to really focus on the people who are most likely to buy the product. Because of the vast number of products on the market, most of our efforts are spent against specific competitors. We want to win market share in a particular price category or region. We have to fish where the fishermen are, and to be successful we have to be better than the other fisherman.

Here are some simple guidelines that can help you win that battle.

Demographics: This is the study of who they are and where to find them. If we can understand our audiences better than the competition, then we will have an obvious advantage. While there are many sources of good information about your consumers, many companies overlook the most obvious source. Because you have direct contact with your consumers, this contact can be used to build a statistical database that will allow you to fine tune your marketing and public relations efforts. Remember, it is interesting to compile data on wine drinkers, but what is really interesting is why YOUR customers choose your products instead of (or more often, in addition to) your competitors'. Most companies have never done the basic research to determine this. You should have a basic script that asks a series of questions of every customer (or every tenth customer) who calls or visits you. And you should use this information to develop programs to reach the customers where they are most likely to live, and then build on the perceived strengths of your company and your products.

In short, you really ought to ask the fish where you can find more of them.

Getting them to act: Not just reaching them, but reaching their souls. Obviously, knowing how to focus your efforts on specific media or specific regions is very helpful. It allows you to use the rifle shot approach to public relations, instead of the shotgun approach. Equally important is knowing what kind of approach will convince them. You may be surprised to learn that most of your customers have no idea about the complex organisms that give flavor to your cheeses, and simply like you because there is a dog on the label. That's important information to have before you commit to a major new public relations program focusing on the various strains of organisms and how they affect what you make. To continue with our fish analogy, you also ought to ask them what bait they prefer, and why.

How to get out front: Everyone loves a leader. If there is one truism of the American market, it is that Americans love to be on the winning side. The good news is that this ties in directly with your search for a key marketing message that will clearly encapsulate your company in a few words. Know where the whole market is going. Know what the trends are. Know what consumers really want. Then tell them how you are leading the way in that direction. If you are not leading the way, then you should look for ways to change that. And you really should ask your entire team what you ARE doing. Are you following? There are few successful companies in the world who have long-term business plans calling for following everyone else. Are you marching to a different drummer? Why? Are there customers who want that? How are they different from the rest of the consumers of the world? If you don't know, then you can't really do effective public relations. If you cannot answer these basic questions, then go back your business plan and review it. It has a flaw, and you have a problem.

Stand by your customers: Right next to them. With so many artisan producers across the country, competition in this business has never been tougher, and it is not always possible to win customers just on the basis of your products. After all, for most consumers, food is only one of many interests—often below movies, music or favorite recreational activities. The solution is simple. Build a relationship between your company and a key element in your customers' lives. You can't be all things to all people, but if you become known as the company that really supports the opera, soap box derbies, or the preservation of the rare Venezuelan cactus, then you will have a group of consumers who know about you and know that you share their values and concerns. Ideally, the cause you select will have its own newsletter or other medium, one that you can use to deliver a direct message to the members, with virtually no competition from others. That is a goal well worth pursuing, for obvious reasons.

How can you find the perfect match between you and your customers? If you don't know the answer to that question now, you haven't been paying attention.

Get focused: I often like to envision all of those potential customers in a huge stadium. On the field in front of the crowd are all of the competitive artisan producers. There are huge crowds of us on the field. You are in that crowd, and you can see just exactly how hard it is to get the attention of the crowd. I bet your mom didn't tell you about this.

One solution is to be one of the biggest players on the field, but that won't work for us, because we're focused on the other end of the spectrum. If you are selling millions and millions of dollars of product, you are going to stand out, even on that crowded field, and the huge audience in the stadium will certainly be aware of what you are doing. Nice work.

But most of us don't fall into that category. And many, many artisan producers are so small that it is easy to imagine them getting trampled to death in the crush. You don't want to be one of those.

You obviously need to stand out, both to gain the attention of the audience and to make sure that those big boys don't step on you. That means doing something different, wearing brighter clothes, dancing wildly in the end zone, hanging from the goal posts, or carrying a sign over your head. There's only one problem with those strategies: every other company is trying to do the same thing.

You could, if you were very clever, try to appeal to just a few of those millions in the audience. You don't need to capture the attention of all of them—you only need a small portion of them. We've all seen this in a stadium. A part of the crowd suddenly comes to life, and the rest of the stadium wonders exactly what happened. So how do you play to only a section of the stands?

Now it's time to start thinking about that stadium in all its glory. Think about where people are sitting. There are the true fans who sit right down close to the field because they love to see the players up close. There are the cheap seats, full of people who love the game, or the team, but not quite ready to mortgage the farm to enjoy the show. And then there are those luxury boxes, often owned or used by people who may not know as much about the game as the most dedicated fans—but at least you know they have the money to afford your product. How do you play to them?

This is the classic dilemma for lifestyle PR. It is certainly glamorous. There is something quite rewarding about seeing your product in the showrooms of Ferrari, Fendi, Dolce & Gabbana, Maserati, etc. From a lifestyle PR perspective, it is a true Home Run.

But there is something we always notice at those sorts of events: many of the people in those elegant showrooms are not all that interested in what they are eating and drinking. You may be reaching exactly the target market of luxury…but that doesn't mean you are going to sell a lot more product. And the world of PR is full of these sorts of efforts and opportunities.

Then we come to the Arts. These are more likely to include our target consumers, and I regularly try to develop strategic alliances with everyone from major museums to the world of music for some of my clients. But museums are almost always non-profit, and need money even more than artisan producers do! Musicians are a really interesting option, but remember that people who like Etta James may not like The Kronos Quartet. Can you afford to work with a group that might alienate some of your customers?

It's a risk/reward equation. If there is little risk that the musician will offend your existing customers, then some kind of alliance might well be worth it—particularly if the musician allows you to meet and make friends with a whole new audience, a part of that stadium that would otherwise never know you are alive.

But if those new customers come at the cost of losing your existing customers, it's not such a great idea after all. A drug-crazed rapper who curses anyone over the age of twenty-nine might not be an ideal partner for you, unless your brand has a pretty distinctive focus.

Geography

One solution is to play to the part of the market that is closest to you. The section of the stadium that is right in front of you will be able to see you more clearly, and so it makes sense to play to them. In terms of PR, this means that you should make darn sure that you have covered your bases with your local audiences: not just customers in your area, but the local papers also, should hear from you on a regular basis. Local restaurants and hotels, even if they don't sell your products, should know that they can recommend you to tourists. Local officials should know who you are and understand what you are doing. That's good basic PR, and it's amazing how often local companies neglect this.

If you are likely to travel to another region on a regular basis, make that area another focus of your efforts. Next time you visit Grandma in the woods, or your daughter at college, start making the connection you need to tell your story. Sign up a local distributor. Stop in at a few stores and restaurants, and sell. And once you've done that, tell your story to the local paper. In other words, play to that part of the crowd as well. The first time it will be hard, but each successive visit will get easier and more effective.

Taking Care of Your Fences

If you've read this far, you know that I have a rather simplistic but effective definition of Public Relations: the relations you have with the various publics of your brand. But there are so many other publics that you need on your side, and most small companies do a really bad job of managing those relationships. Let's talk about three of them that can really make a difference in your life.

Local Officials

Even in the Napa Valley (perhaps especially in the Napa Valley!) local regulations concerning use permits, land policies, business taxation and traffic patterns are major topics of local concern. These topics directly affect the way that you run your company.

It is critical that local officials understand what you do, and why it is important to the local economy. It's also important for them to understand how you are playing a role in the larger community, and how your business positively affects their town or county. They aren't going to find out if you don't tell them. You should have a plan to reach their local officials with a steady stream of helpful information about these topics. More importantly, you should have a plan to develop personal and direct relationships with the elected officials in their community. Letters to the editor and Facebook posts are all well and good, but face time beats Facebook every single time. Meet with them, talk to them, try to understand their goals, and try to explain how you can help the community achieve them.

And no, you can't hope that someone else can do this for you. It's your company, and therefore it's your business.

Good Neighbors

Of course, if you are currently experiencing some complicated relationships with your local officials, it's probably because one or more of your neighbors has complained about you. Remember your list of the different publics you made? Your neighbors should be pretty high on that list of your publics.

Let's face it: People are never happy to see a new parking lot spring up next door to their house, especially if it means that there will be a lot of cars in it every day. And when those cars bring people who laugh, talk loudly, go to concerts, and picnic on the property next door, it's even worse.

If I were your neighbor, I might complain about it!

What's the solution? You need a plan. You should develop a complete communications plan for your neighbors. Invite them to see what you are doing and ask them what they think. Communication, despite what we see from many politicians on TV, is a two-way street. Start by asking questions and listening to their answers. Many times, you will be able to address their concerns directly, person to person, so that these concerns never make it to the local city council.

Part of your plan should include inviting your neighbors to visit you, and meet you. But don't stop there. Continue to reach out to your neighbors on a regular basis. With the right approach from you, they can become some of your strongest brand ambassadors.

Local Paper Makes Good

And while we're at it, let's put in a kind word for the reporters/bloggers/announcers at your local newspapers, magazines, websites and other media. While their circulation may be more limited, they often have a serious impact in your own backyard. The next time you see the staff writer for the local paper, I would suggest saying hello. The foundation that you lay today will be very important when the journalist calls about something important to you. If you don't run into them, make a plan to meet them so that you can do this. After all, when fresh-faced young college grads get out of school, they generally don't get offered jobs for the *Washington Post*. Most of them start at very small local publications—and some go on to much bigger and better things. Meet them now, when they live and work next door to you.

By the way, if you ever look at a major news story, you will note that the footnote at the end often mentions contributors to the story. Some of those people are local writers who may have been covering the story, or the industry, for years—local reporters for local papers.

This also has an effect on your internet Search Engine Optimization. As these publications put their content on the web, the search engines find it and put it near the top of your "Google" listings. So consumers who use search engines to find you on the Web will find lots of independent, third-party articles about you and your products. That's good. Even better, you will find that many mainstream journalists (TV, radio, and print) use these same techniques. They search the internet, find these articles, and may even contact the authors to discuss what they know and what they learned.

Local Knowledge Works Both Ways

One of the most powerful wine writers in the world once told me that he got a lot of great story ideas from talking to the spouses of his neighbors at the grocery store. While the owner might well try to convey one story or one image to him, the word on the street from those who worked there was telling a different tale altogether. He was smart enough to listen to both.

For all the effort we put into managing our image on a national basis, we often overlook the local people who see us every day. While we would never appear in front of a gala dinner in New York in sweats, the locals in our town see us at the supermarket, the bank, and the gym. And they remember us.

Your local taxi drivers, restaurant waitresses, or hotel concierges are all capable of telling stories about their neighborhood, and those stories may not be the same versions that we work so hard to develop with the marketing and sales team. It pays to make sure that when you communicate something to your key audiences, you don't forget that one of those audiences is your local community.

Do it right, and they will appreciate your efforts and respect your honesty. Do it poorly, and they will take great delight in telling all of their friends, neighbors, and contacts about the juicy details—details which may not be true, but which certainly make the story more interesting.

CHAPTER 4

WHY PR? ADVERTISING, PUBLIC RELATIONS, AND OTHER EFFECTIVE MESSAGE DELIVERY SYSTEMS

Advertising vs. PR: Which Is Best for You?

Yes, I admit it; I have a bias here. But I also run a company that provides both advertising and public relations services to our clients. And some of our clients focus almost completely on advertising—with our blessing. So which is best for you?

Well, let's start with a couple of basic assumptions:

1. You have a limited budget. In the world of artisan food and beverages, we simply don't have the kind of money to play with the big boys. It may seem as if you have a lot of product to sell, but compared to industrial giants like Coca-Cola, Budweiser, and Kraft, your budget doesn't even reach the level of a rounding error. Most packaged goods companies would laugh out loud at our budgets. They would tell you that we don't have the volume, revenue or budgets to really tackle national advertising campaigns. In terms that the rest of the world understands, you have a very limited budget.

2. You often have a national sales target. Yes, I know that you sell a lot of your product locally, but as you grow, you'll need to support that growth in other markets. And you are trying to do this with a limited budget. See #1 above.

3. In advertising, frequency is the only way to make sure people get your message. So you have to run lots of ads over a period of time, and you have to do this in several major markets. And you are trying to do this on a limited budget. See #1 above.

The Codfish lays ten thousand eggs
The homely hen lays one
The codfish never cackles
To tell you what she's done.
And so we scorn the codfish
While the humble hen we prize
Which only goes to show you
It pays to advertise.

Well, yes and no.

What's Right About Advertising?

Advertising can be an incredibly powerful weapon. A really well done creative campaign can really capture the attention of every level of the market, from distributors and retailers right through to the consumer. It can create a positive image for your company that will sell product and resist a huge amount of damage. Really good ad campaigns can even become news in their own right—how many times have you heard someone say, "Oh, I love those ads!"

Of course, loving the ads and buying the products are two different things. All too often the ads that most people remember are ones that don't really deliver the complete brand message—because they have sacrificed brand message for entertainment. And they will ultimately fall short of the goal because of this. Our world is full of memorable ad campaigns for companies that went bankrupt because their sales did not improve. I hate it when that happens!

But the perfect ad campaign can have a huge positive effect. In the end it can achieve one of those great marketing goals: it can help you own a word in the buyer's mind. Coke is IT. Nike says, "Just do it!"

Of course, such advertising campaigns usually cost a lot of money, both for the creative work (there is no such thing as a great, cheap, creative agency) and for the media placement itself. Remember what advertising icon Hal Riney said about media placement: "In advertising, less isn't more, it's less."

If you don't have the money to get the ad placed everywhere it needs to be seen, and seen with great frequency by the target market, then you can't really expect it to generate the kind of success you would like. And every year we see ad campaigns that fail simply because the company doesn't plan to spend the money necessary for the market to see the ads. Repetition is the key. Repetition costs money.

See #1 above.

And I know that every single publication on the face of the planet will deny this, but I can assure you that in the right circumstances, and with the right publisher, a significant advertising campaign can help buy editorial coverage.

Cover your ears now, as you hear the screams of editorial departments throughout the country denying this vociferously.

The truth is that no editor likes to get a phone call from an advertising client (or the publisher, forwarding the message) asking for a special feature article in return for a major new ad placement contract. Most resist the idea, with varying degrees of success.

At the same time, if that editor is doing an article on foods from a certain region, and one of the producers in that region is a major advertiser, I can assure you that the editorial staff will make every effort to taste the products from that advertiser. They may even taste them with a slightly less critical palate—or taste more products than from other producers. In other cases, they may even take advantage of the relationship they have with the advertiser to get an extra quote, another photo, or a sidebar story.

On the defensive side, many times major advertisers will get advance notice about a negative story, and may even be given more opportunity to respond to their critics than a non-advertiser would get. It's the way the game is played.

And some publications that will remain nameless (would you give out the names and locations of your best secret trout streams?) will take direct input from an advertiser, and print long and large feature stories about those companies. Some will not print feature stories about any company that does NOT advertise. Don't say you weren't warned. As one publisher put it to me, "Why would I write about the producer you are pitching, when I could write about someone who advertises with me?"

Those are all advantages of advertising. Don't overlook them.

If you don't have the budget to undertake a major national advertising campaign, don't give up all hope. Even small listings in the classified ads can help you get your message out. And they will also keep your name in the spotlight, and show your flag to customers who are ready to buy. That's not a bad idea. I remember one campaign in a leading magazine that simply asked, "Want to find out who won the most medals in competitions last year? Call this number: 800- *** ****." Clever. Because when you called the number, you got the office of the company who placed the ad.

Finally, I have to note here that many of what we consider to be consumer magazines are really more influential with the trade than with consumers. And a solid and well-funded advertising campaign can play a key role in distributor support. It is tangible evidence that you are supporting your brand in their markets, and that is pretty powerful stuff—provided you are doing better, and more extensively, than your competition.

You did remember your competition, didn't you? If you are going to compete against them, you have to compete at every level, including advertising. And if you are a small company, remember that your ads have to compete against the big boys in size, creative content, and frequency. That's not usually a challenge small artisan producers can ever meet.

Advertising As a Medium

One of my all-time favorite quotes from the world of marketing comes from Lord Leverhulme. Concerned about his advertising budget, and knowing that the ads were never as perfectly targeted as he would like, he said, "I know that half the money I spend on advertising is wasted, and the trouble is I don't know which half."

Ain't that the truth?

Advertising does allow you to get your message to the audience. While public relations programs are far more sensitive to the turn of events in the news, once you have paid your money, your ad will appear in the publication just when you expect it to—and it will appear just the way you drew it up. Your message, the way you wrote it, and delivered to the publication's readers exactly when you specified.

It's exactly as if they gave you a page in the magazine to say anything that you wanted. In fact, that's exactly what they did. You can't say that about a PR campaign.

On the other hand, there are some drawbacks to advertising in general, and some very specific challenges to advertising in the wine industry.

What Is Wrong with Advertising?

For artisan producers, most advertising is simply not cost-effective. We don't have the dollars to go after national campaigns, or anything close. While cosmetics and car companies can advertise on national TV, we don't have the budget for that. And the ugly fact about artisan food and drink in general is that not enough people in the U.S. buy it. Forget about half of Lord Leverhulme's budget being wasted—if you are advertising wine on national TV, you are lucky if only fifty percent of your budget is being spent reaching people who aren't interested in artisanal products. Given your budget, that hurts.

Even with the most sophisticated media analysis, it is tough to come up with a radio or television show that will deliver an audience that is composed of people who really focus on artisanal products on a regular basis. The same is true for newspapers, general interest magazines, and the kind of lifestyle publications that feature ads for all sorts of other aspirational purchases.

Which means that in our business, our list of potentially targeted publications is pretty small. And we all know most of them by name. It is pretty safe to assume that the readers of *Wine Spectator, Wine Enthusiast,* and *Wine & Spirits* are interested in wine.

Now the question we have to ask is, "Does advertising in those magazines convince readers to buy our products?"

Well, yes and no.

Such advertising can encourage more activity from retailers and distributors, and that will certainly increase sales. But there is also an odd little streak in many consumers in this country that resists advertising at almost every level. In one way or the other, these consumers seem to say, "If a company advertises, then it is too big to make good products." They actually resist buying things from companies that advertise. And while those consumers tend to buy at the higher end of the market, I suspect that most of the readers of this book are aiming much of their marketing communications directly at those very consumers.

A second concern about advertising is that any customer who can be won over to your products by your ads can just as easily be lost to a competitor by their, better ads. And since many smaller companies simply can't afford the kind of very professional advertising of their larger competitors, they are at a huge disadvantage. They don't have the money to create really memorable, effective advertising, and they don't have the budget to slather those ads all over the top magazines. In a battle of perceptions, these smaller producers are trying to fight a war with a pitchfork and a peashooter.

Even larger companies run certain risks by spending too many of their dollars on national ad campaigns. In a wine world that is constantly in flux, a national ad campaign can force a company into a static position, defending a hopeless cause while the rest of the industry has moved on. And even worse are those who invest heavily in personality ads, only to see the key personnel leave or pass away, leaving the marketing message completely at sea.

Sadly, when it comes to advertising, one of the biggest challenges of all is that you have no third party credibility. What you say about yourself is often quite open to debate in the eyes and ears of the buying public. Even worse, they can even react with disagreement or even ridicule in the right (wrong?) situation. That is really ugly.

This resistance to advertising messages is captured in some sense by Michael Phillips & Salli Rasberry, in their book *Marketing Without Advertising*. They are obviously not big supporters of advertising, and they warn consumers against taking any advertising claims too seriously: "We've all seen these (popular ad) slogans for so many years, and they're so familiar, that you have to concentrate to even hear them and pay attention to understand why they are either hype or simply not true."

That's not exactly the response you are hoping to get to your carefully crafted, and extensively placed advertising campaign!

Of course, it would be easy to make your ads more believable by quoting independent third parties. But in the end, those kinds of ads start to look an awful lot like a supermarket shelf, where every tiny producer has a rave review. There is no product differentiation, and there is no unique selling proposition to the consumer. Given that you are spending a lot of money to get this message in front of the consumers, you really ought to be able to explain how and why you are different.

All too often, when small companies start to think about marketing, they think about advertising first. They put an inordinately large portion of their budget into the advertising bucket. They know it is expensive, and they really want to make sure they have enough money to do it well. The only problem is, they don't really know what the goal of that advertising is. If you carefully define what your expectations for your advertising are, then you will quickly realize exactly what kind of advertising is cost-effective, and what kind is simply a massive drain on your finances, with no real hope of return on investment.

What is the solution? Well, I did list a few things that advertising can do successfully for you above. They are solid techniques, and represent legitimate goals for the marketing programs for any company. Combined with an effective campaign integrating public relations, promotions, and direct marketing, they can play a key role in making a company successful.

And if you are really worried about carefully targeting your advertising, take a look at some of the opportunities on the internet. You can buy key search words to pre-select who sees your ads (e.g., only those who type in "craft cheeses" in their Google searches) to make sure that you reach only interested readers. That would seem to be a pretty foolproof system, but it's not. In the example above, there is every reason to believe that you are going to have at least some of those people looking for Kraft cheeses, and spelling it wrong!

As many internet retailers will tell you, the on-line shopper is often someone who is only interested in low prices. If you reach that audience, you may find that they are only interested in your least expensive options ... and not in your artisanal quality. That's not an ideal target market. Then again, the costs for these kinds of campaigns are quite low compared to traditional print or broadcast media advertising.

There are certainly ways to tell your story to these on-line searchers, but there is some doubt as to whether they will become your long-time customers. After all, they have very little invested in your brand at that point. They just happened upon it (thanks to your keyword advertising) as they wandered through across the Web. That's a very different kind of customer than one who walks in your door. It would take something quite sensational to really grab their attention.

In the end analysis, advertising is one of many different options to deliver your key message to your target audience. No one option will be perfect for any producer. But unless you have a larger budget than more artisanal companies have at their disposal, advertising is a lot like high proof liquor: A small amount is probably all you need.

CHAPTER 5

CLASSICAL PR—GETTING THE MEDIA TO TELL YOUR STORY

Any good communications campaign can be broken down into three basic elements: the message, the audience, and the delivery system. What do you want to say? Whom do you want to receive it? And how are you going to make sure it gets through? The media play a key role, because they can become the delivery system for your message. In fact, if you reach the right writer with the right story, you can talk to one good journalist and get them to share your story with more than a million readers. That's really efficient marketing communications.

But in some ways, one of the biggest challenges is figuring out how to get the media to really get excited about your message. Which brings us to the obvious question:

What Do Writers Want?

There are seemingly hundreds of books on the shelves right now about what women want, or what men want. The basis for most of these books is simple: Most people are too shy, too inhibited, or too intimidated to ask for what they really want. So we read books to try and understand the other people in our lives.

That isn't the problem with most media. Most writers are pretty darn open about what they want. They want good stories that really touch the human heart. They want hard data that sheds light on new trends or developments in the industry. That's news. They want real news, and they want great accounts of people that put that news into a human perspective. That's stories.

The media wants news and it wants stories.

News is anything that has an impact on the way we live, and is timely. A local journalist once asked me the perfect question to help me understand the difference. When I called him to pitch a story, he asked if I could wait and talk to him tomorrow. I said that it could wait—and he then informed me that what I had was not news. News can't wait. It has to make it to press immediately. Most of us in our business don't have news. That's OK. We usually have stories.

So what's a story? Stories are about people, not about things. That's because stories need characters, and they need dramatic tension. That means a plot. A good story has to invite us to go along, to follow the main character on a quest or a challenge, so that we can see if he wins or loses. That's a story. Making cheese isn't a story. Facing many challenges and overcoming them is a story.

I'd like to suggest a simple test here. If you are telling how you make your product, you are not telling a story. If you are telling WHY you make your product, there's a much greater chance that you will be telling a story—about motivation, about personal growth, and about passion.

Tell that story.

That's all they want. Why is it so hard for us to give that to them? Instead we tend to focus on the minutiae of production, resulting in sheer unadulterated boredom. Sadly, artisan producers are the perfect soil for that particular crop.

Hard data is hard to come by, and everyone is working off the same figures. Human interest stories? Well, yes, every artisan thinks that his story is special, but there are few that stand up to a comparison with the kind of emotional impact that we see every day on the news. Hard news? You can probably count the times that an artisan producer will be on the front page of any newspaper in any year on one hand. We just don't have the numbers, widespread appeal, or sensationalism that is going to get us front-page coverage.

So right off the bat, we need to be honest about our expectations. We need to recognize that we are fighting for a small piece of the media pie.

And we need to recognize that we do not have the kinds of big stories that are going to get national coverage. When we do, it's probably going to be because someone died.

That doesn't mean that we should give up hope, or stop trying. It does mean that when we don't have a major pitch to make, we need to do the rest of our job really well. We need to fight for every word, every mention, and every column inch. And we need to do that in the most professional way possible. In simple terms, we need to do the best possible job of supporting our media contacts.

Just the Facts, Ma'am

First of all, writers often call with a simple request for information. They are looking for the latest sales figures for a brand or category, pricings, or historical dates to fill out a story. Our job, as public relations professionals, is to get them that information, and to do it as conveniently as possible for the media.

N.B. Such requests are rarely a good opportunity to try and pitch a major story to a writer. When a writer calls for pricing information about your current products, please don't make him or her sit through a twenty-minute pitch on sustainability practices in your business. See Chapter 8 for a more specific discussion of media training.

Think of your role in this situation as customer service. When you call a store to ask when they are open, you really resent sitting through a twenty-minute sales presentation on electronics, don't you? Why should the media be any different?

This doesn't mean you shouldn't take advantage of the fact that you have the writer on the phone. It means that you should see the issue from their perspective. When they call, first give them the price of the product. Then ask them if they have time to chat about another story idea. If they do, then go full speed ahead. If they don't, ask them for a good time to follow up with a longer discussion. That way you will give them what they want, and still leave the door open for the longer discussion.

What happens when a writer calls for information, and you don't have a story to pitch? Shame on you—you should always have a story to pitch. In fact, if Eric Asimov called you from the *New York Times*, you should have at least one story to pitch about every product you represent. And you should be prepared to give that pitch very professionally on a moment's notice. That's the job.

Just don't confuse that job with the job of serving the media. If all you do is pitch, and you don't respond to what the media wants, you will find yourself getting damn few phone calls from writers. That is a bad thing.

Say It with Style

The second reason that the media calls us is to get a truly memorable quote for a story. You know the situation: a brewer in Egypt has been found guilty of clarifying his beer with the dust from ancient mummies, and you've got a journalist on the phone who wants to know what the American craft brewing industry thinks of this practice.

What Do You Do Next?

Well, this is a great time to think strategically. Ask yourself a few simple questions:

1. How does this story help me tell my message about my company? If you can use this opportunity to tell that story about sustainability ("We would never condone such practices, because at Moffitt Brewery we are committed to making beer in a sustainable way for this generation and for all future generations of Americans"), then by all means go for it. It is simply an opportunity to get your prime message in front of the audience, and that is what you are paid to do.

2. Does this story have the potential to damage my company or brand by association? If so, run like the wind. Do NOT answer questions that are posed with an unacceptable premise, and do NOT answer questions that attempt to put you in the position of answering a question about unethical or negative practices for the entire industry. That is not your job, and it will only hurt you. Remember when you were told that all coverage is good coverage,

as long as they spell your name right? Well, we can all think of recent stories where that just isn't true.

And I hate to say it, but sometimes it is hard to tell what kind of story the journalist is writing. How do you find out? First of all, by knowing your writers, and reading what they write. Secondly, by asking a few questions of your own. Whom has the writer interviewed so far? What seems to be the industry response? By asking away, you may be able to get a few clues as to the perspective, or even bias, of the writer. That should influence your decision strongly.

3. Is there a way to answer this question in a way that will be really memorable? The media doesn't just want an opinion; they want a real quote, something that they can run as a pull quote in a box inside the story. They want it to be concise, full of impact, and maybe just a bit funny. Remember that story about the mummy? "We would never condone such practices, because at Moffitt Brewery we are committed to making beer in a sustainable way for this generation and for all future generations of Americans. My mother would be turning over in her grave if we did this!"

I guarantee the last part of that quote would get printed.

ASAP

Contrary to what most businesspeople seem to think, deadlines are not negotiable. When a writer calls and asks for information, he or she usually lets you know what kind of timeline they have. And if they don't tell you, ask for it. This is critical for two reasons.

First of all, if they are really on a tight deadline, you need to do some immediate triage. How much of the information can you get them, and how quickly can you get it to them? What parts of that information are proprietary, and what hoops will you have to jump through in order to release it? It is a very simple equation: If you cannot get them some solid, valuable information before their deadline, you will not be in that story. Period.

And unless I am seriously mistaken, your job is to get your company or brand into the stories that are written. When a journalist calls, your reaction should be to call all hands on deck, and everyone to battle stations, and provide them an immediate response with everything you can possibly offer to make the story a good one.

If you do that, you will get another call from that writer. That's the goal.

On the other hand, if the writer tells you that the deadline is a week away, that gives you time to put together a more carefully considered and crafted response. You can afford to do a little research, perhaps more so than the writer. The information you uncover and provide will make a big difference in the story. It will also greatly enhance your standing in the eyes of the writer. That's a good thing.

You can also take some time to really craft your response to make it as strong, memorable, and interesting as possible. Develop those quotes, and write those copy points in a way that will get you featured in the pull quote, not buried in the nineteenth paragraph on page three. You may even have time to pitch your winemaker or principal as a good interview on the subject. And that might get you more than just a pull quote—it might get you a sidebar, or even a photo or label in the main story.

But be careful here. Response time is absolutely critical to your success with the media, but it should never keep you from asking the questions above. If you don't have a clear idea of what the story is about, how the writer is approaching the topic, and what the potential risks and opportunities are for your company, then a quick response time will only serve to make the potential for your professional death quicker. It still won't be painless.

As a hypothetical note, if a writer ever calls to ask why many consumers have mistaken a $1 bottle of Thompson Seedless Wine for a $39 bottle of high-end Chardonnay, you do NOT want to be the one member of the industry to be quoted about how hard it is to tell the difference in a blind tasting. Because I can guarantee that the writer will make you the butt of a series of pointed comments about wine marketing, pricing, and your own ability to taste wine. And yes, they will spell your name right. They may even include a photo or a label reproduction in the story. That's not coverage you want to encourage.

Be the "Go To" Source, Whatever the Question

We have a standard policy at Balzac: Whenever a writer calls with a question, we will get them the answer. We will do it quickly, efficiently, and accurately. And we will do it even when the question is about a brand or wine that we do not represent.

Why?

Because we have worked long and hard to build our reputation and relationships with the media. They know they can call us in any situation, and we will get them the information they need. That includes situations in which the wineries in question are not our clients.

We do it because we want them to call us every time they have a question. We want them to call us first. And we want them to know, year after year, that we are the best single source for them and their stories.

It seems to work.

The Face of the News: Meeting the Media: Game, Set and Match

In the best of all possible worlds, when a journalist calls you about a story, you will not only see the opportunity to present a few key facts in an effective way; you will also see a chance to position one of the members of your management team in a very positive light in the story. And if you do this just right, you may even get them the chance to be interviewed in depth for the story.

Of course, the first step is to pitch your spokesperson as the ideal interview subject. This means that you have to know enough about the topic to know what the key issues are, and how to document your spokesperson's leadership on these issues. This is where playing an active role in an industry trade association can really pay off, as the president of a trade association automatically has more credibility that any single company spokesperson.

If the goal of our public relations campaign is to get our story into widespread distribution, then one of our key strategies needs to be to the key appropriate media. We tell our story to them, they re-tell it to a much larger (and hopefully accurately targeted) audience. That's smart PR.

But the media is not without its risks. While their third party endorsements add credibility to our message, we can't always be sure that the media will tell our story the way we want it told. One place that we immediately see the potential for failure is in the interview process. Unless you and the journalist are on exactly the same page, things can turn out quite differently from what you plan or expect.

And that should make you nervous.

What can be done to maximize your potential for success? I like to describe a media interview as a tennis match—each question is a chance to hit the ball back over the net. But there is a big difference between tennis and an interview. In an interview, the writer is both your opponent and the umpire: He or she gets to set the rules and make all the calls.

How can you possibly win in that situation? The answer is simple. Your job isn't to win—it's to help the journalist win in a way that also helps you get your story out. If you think your job is to win, you are going to lose.

Know Your Opponent

A journalist at an interview isn't really playing against you, so it's a bit unfair to call him or her an opponent. But make no mistake: the journalist has a goal for the interview, and it is not the same as your goal. If you don't know what the journalist wants, there is no way that you can help him or her achieve that goal. It's as if you are playing singles, and the writer is playing doubles: not a good match.

So what does the journalist want? A good story for his or her readers. And let's be honest, on this point most winemakers are really not very good. You may know what makes a great cheese, but that doesn't mean you know how to tell a good story. The writer does. You have to read a few articles that the writer has published in the last few weeks or months, so that you can get a good idea of what he or she thinks is a good story. That's what you have to deliver with every answer.

It's a critical step. Do not assume that your story is interesting to everyone. Some writers actively campaign against expensive products, flavored beers, or even products in a certain style or character. Some writers love human interest stories, and some think such stories are a distraction from the "real" business. If you don't know this in advance, then every question becomes a landmine. And your responses only serve to turn the writer down the wrong path.

Train for the Match

The fact that you are an artisan producer does not make you a professional spokesperson. Writers are professional interviewers. You are at an obvious disadvantage. The solution is to hire a professional coach who can get you up to speed on how the game is played at the top level.

It takes time and skill to become a good interviewee, and it's your job to get good at it. A media trainer can help you understand the process, give you the kind of practice that you need to feel comfortable, and help you prepare for each writer's questions and style. You will also need to train hard for the main event—practicing your skills on a regular basis so that you are ready and able to take advantage of any interview opportunity, no matter when or how it appears.

Practice, Practice, Practice

You can't learn to play tennis in a day, and you can't learn to give good interviews in a day, either. The only way you can get better is to practice, and the only way you can stay in top form is to practice regularly. Find time to do that, either in the tasting room or at wine festivals, and make sure that you bring in a professional to work with you every once in a while, just to keep you at the top of your game.

The techniques above are not only helpful for meetings with journalists; they can also improve your communications skills for the rest of your life. And that's a very good thing.

How Do You Know If You Did A Good Job?

Forget spelling your name right. That's only the very first step. The only good coverage is coverage that captures your key marketing message, front and center.

We all spend huge amounts of our time trying to gain the attention of the media. After all, the real challenge in Public Relations is getting our story in front of a writer who will write about it. Isn't it? That's why we all spend so much time focusing on our media contacts—those key writers who will write whatever we tell them, every time.

Sadly, I don't know any writers like that. I only know writers who want good stories. When I talk to the media, they want solid information; they want it quickly and accurately, and they usually prefer it if I can give it to them in a pithy quote.

Those pithy quotes are hard to come by.

I have found that the best way to get my clients to agree to media training is to ask them the very tough questions. When they have to think about the answers, I point out the reasons that we would like to save them from some of that pain. And they usually agree.

Not every business owner is a glib and clever speaker, able to deliver that great quote, that great story, or that convincing explanation.

If that's true of your company, then you have two options: You can hire a professional spokesperson, either a Public Relations pro or a well-known expert, and let them do the talking, or you can trust your PR to materials that provide the kinds of quotes and information that the media needs to do their job for you.

If you do hire the professional spokesperson, be aware that they bring both expertise and risks (you don't want your brewery spokesperson to get arrested for a DUI). And even after hiring a spokesperson, you will need to provide him or her with the information and quotes you want them to deliver.

But that's the next chapter.

CHAPTER 6

GETTING THE MESSAGE RIGHT

Getting the message right: It has to be true. It has to be evocative. It has to be important to those who hear it. Your aim should be to seduce the reader, not impress her. Remember that you want her to fall in love, not come to an intellectual conclusion. And forget the hocus pocus.

The Words Matter

Like most things in life, public relations is about ten percent inspiration and ninety percent perspiration. For every brilliant stroke of genius that garners massive media coverage, there are probably hundreds of hours of meticulous grunt work to make sure that all the landmines are eliminated and all the avenues of success are fully exploited. There is no such thing as the perfect idea that sells itself.

And for every ten great ideas that comes up in a brainstorming session, nine of them are going to get eliminated somewhere down the line simply because they are too darn difficult (or expensive) to execute in a way that will fully realize their potential. In the immortal philosophy of our business: Cheap, quick, good…Pick two!

Those are the facts of life, and they underscore how really critical it is to craft the language of a public relations program as carefully as possible. In the intensely competitive world of media management, a single word or phrase can make the difference between success and failure. It can be the difference between major media coverage and a lone voice, unheard in the wilderness.

Say the Magic Word

The words you use in your press releases and interviews have to accomplish two not-very-related goals. On the one hand, those words must perfectly capture the essence of your brand message, and make that message clear beyond all doubt to all who read them. And on the other hand, those words must capture the imagination and attention of a media that is completely saturated with the traditional messages of quality and integrity.

Do you want to stand out from the crowd? Yes. Do you want be to known for the quality of your products? Yes. But so does everybody else. Talking about the quality of your cheeses won't attract much attention— you will be one of a thousand voices singing the same basic music and lyrics. So what can you do about this? Sadly, dancing is rarely an option!

It's not really hard to stand out from the crowd. All you have to do is be very different. But if everyone else is talking about quality, talking about something different may not help you sell your product. After all, what attracts people to artisan products is quality, and our customers are rightly suspicious of those who somehow seem to downplay the quality of what they make.

This is where using the perfect word or phrase can get you attention above and beyond the facts of the case.

Years ago, in a story that was included in Paul Franson and Harvey Posert's book *Spinning the Bottle*, we responded to a rainstorm during the Napa Valley grape harvest by calling the media and talking about the impact this would have on the quality of the wines. Weather is always news, but this wasn't anything that got the media excited. They had better angles to that story, and they told us so. That all changed when one of my employees described how our client was using helicopters in the vineyards to "blow dry" the vines. Suddenly we had three news crews (all in helicopters!) covering the story for a national news audience.

The difference? A turn of phrase that caught the attention of an otherwise tired and sated media audience. They knew that the very same phrase would capture the imagination (and the sense of humor) of their own audiences. As good middlemen for the news, they knew this was a product that would sell. And it did.

When discussing this anecdote, it is important to note that the use of helicopters to dry vineyards was not new or even unusual at that time. But the media had never covered it, so it was news to them. And that is a rule that always bears remembering in this business: Being first is not the same as being the first to be recognized. Being the first to be recognized is usually a lot better.

Improve the Story

Every press release you write should be carefully crafted to make the most of every opportunity that is available. It should also be crafted to take advantage of every turn of phrase that can help make the message both memorable and notable. If you never write or see a draft of a press release that makes you nervous, you are not pushing creativity hard enough. Memorable phrases have a price, and sometimes that price is too high. But you have to shop around, and see how far you can go. Otherwise, you might settle for far too little far too often.

Writing press releases is very much like solving a puzzle. You have to make all of the pieces fit, and there is usually only one way to do it. Sometimes you discover that the very best way to fit the pieces together leaves a big hole in the middle. That's when it is time to go back to the client and see what you can do to make this story even better.

One of our clients recently released a wine honoring the memory of Elvis Presley. By timing the release of the wine with the Wine and Spirits Wholesaler Association's national convention in Las Vegas, we were able to give the story a much better spin, and a big boost in interest. After all, who could resist a headline that proclaimed that Elvis was coming to Vegas to launch a new wine?

The story received national attention, and client was delighted that the coverage included mention of the many awards for quality that the wines had won over the past few years. They got their quality story in the news by attaching it to something much more fun and interesting to the media. That is a great recipe for success—and it wouldn't have happened if the wine had been released without the Vegas connection.

Practice, Practice, Practice

Press releases are not the only area where the choice of words is so critical. Media training often has many of the same opportunities for a cleverly turned phrase. If a journalist interviews three or four people for a story, the interviewees who will get quoted the most will be the ones who are most articulate. Does this mean that your spokesperson has to have the ability of Robin Williams to think on his or her feet?

Absolutely not.

(Actually, if the late Robin Williams *were* a spokesperson for one of our programs, I would be terrified. I would be laughing hysterically—but completely terrified. That kind of creativity is like a match in a dynamite factory. Who knows what will happen?!)

What is needed is enough media training for your spokesperson to understand how and when to introduce a few quotable comments in any interview. Rather than being recognized as the undisputed expert on a topic, your spokesperson should aim for a somewhat more attainable goal: someone who can explain the subject in a simple, clear, and memorable way.

Memorable is the key word here. I was once interviewed on NPR about the glut of wines on the market, and in a sidebar conversation, I was asked why there were so many different kinds of wines in the world. I pulled out an old line I had used from my wine education days, and explained that wines were like dinner guests. Sometimes you want to have dinner with Dolly Parton, and sometimes you want to have dinner with Catherine Deneuve. The interviewer laughed, and the rest of the conversation was both friendly and rewarding for us both.

I knew that the line was memorable. I also knew that it wasn't exactly on topic for the larger story of the wine glut. But I was sure that when the rest of the interviews were edited out onto the radio station's floor, this one quote would still be in the story. It was too good to leave out. It made people smile when they heard it, and it did capture that element of variety and choice that is so critical to understanding the wine market.

In the end, they interviewed about eight people for that story, and only three of us actually made it onto the air. The other quotes they used from me allowed me to get my key point across, but I am sure they had a number of other options. What won the day was that single, memorable quote.

Most people don't automatically create great and memorable lines every time they open their mouths. Those of us who teach a lot have an advantage, simply because we get to test so many lines with an audience, and we really get the chance to see which ones work. But even if you don't have that opportunity, your media training should include a few choice phrases that always get used in interviews and speeches. Those are the lines that will get quoted, over and over again.

Some spokespeople resist this kind of training, and insist that it takes away from the real give and take of an interview. I would argue exactly the opposite. There is a reason big name comedians sometimes show up at comedy clubs and perform free of charge. It is not that they are motivated purely by a sense of generously sharing their enormous talent. It is because they know they need the practice, and even with their tremendous experience, they need to get a sense of what really works with the audience.

It's safe to say that your spokesperson is not quite so talented, which would make practice and training more important, rather than less. Insist on it. A key part of that practice is feedback from the audience. If your spokesperson is capably answering every question, and competently delivering every message, that's good. But I begin to worry when a client tells me that he or she is not nervous or excited about an interview. You should have a bit of an edge. You are on stage. And if you can draw attention to a couple of good lines that are really memorable, that's a lot better. To do that, you really have to be on top of your game.

Avoid Trite Lingo

For every artisan product there is an industry argot that works its way through a virtual library of catch phrases. Wines are barrel-fermented, estate-bottled, reserve, unfined and unfiltered. All have had their day in the sun, as have handcrafted microbrews and even such terms as Extra

Virgin Olive Oil. Once used, they became popular. Once popular, they became tired. Once tired, they have become almost completely ignored, or even worse, meaningless. Don't invest huge amounts of your message in such catch phrases. Right now it seems that every artisan product in the world is made with passion. In another two years, that passion will have waned, and we will have a whole new and exciting term. "Intense" may be critical this year, but next year we may well be talking about "elegance" instead of power, and finesse instead of richness.

Your ability to talk about your product in ways that are cleverer than the rest of the market will really pay off.

As you can see from the preceding, catch phrases are frequently technical terms, stemming from some kind of more or less arcane production terminology. I know it's hard to believe, especially since we all spend our lives developing the skills, techniques and artistry to create unique products, but most of our customers care less about how we make the product than about the story behind it. That means talking, and writing, with emotion as well as style.

Wear Your Heart on Your Sleeve

Every journalism instructor quotes Rudyard Kipling at one point or the other, listing the six honest serving men that answer every question the reader may have: what, where, when, why, how, and who. Every press release should provide that information in the first paragraph. Every interview should make sure that information is clearly conveyed. But there is more to the job than just providing information. There is the art of communicating well.

The difference between information and communication is an active one. Information exists. Communication is the process of making sure that someone else understands that information. There is both beauty and art in the successful execution of a communications campaign. The most successful ones capture more than just information; they capture the attention and enthusiasm of the audience.

One of the reasons that my company is named Balzac has to do with that author's ability to communicate. Over the course of his life, Honoré de Balzac wrote more than eighty novels, all of which capture the unique sociology of France during that time period. He was so successful in his studies of French society that his work has been summarized quite famously as *La Comédie Humaine,* The Human Comedy.

In many ways, what Balzac wrote was a perfect sociological study of France. And yet if that were all that he had written, his works would now be largely unknown. By writing that study in the form of fascinating and emotionally charged novels, Balzac reached into the hearts of his readers to communicate the story of the people of France. What began as sociology, in the hands of a literary master, has become one of the foundations of culture in France. He made the information come to life in an utterly memorable way, and is now honored as one of the great masters of French literature.

In some ways, that's what we do for our clients. We take a relatively stale set of facts and information, and by working emotion and interest into the story, we make it something that the media wants to cover, and people want to read. No, it's not brain surgery, but it is a form of art. And now it's your job.

Hocus Pocus

The English use of the term "hocus pocus" goes back hundreds of years. Over the years the meaning has slowly changed, and the term now does a wonderful job of capturing that sense of magic and mystery that surrounds the language of the arcane, while implying that there is something absolutely phony about the whole thing.

Not that the artisan food industry needs to be arcane, or phony. We just choose to be that way all too often!

The history of hocus pocus goes back to the celebration of Mass in Catholic churches. In those early days, the Mass was celebrated in Latin, and the sacramental blessing began with the words *hoc est corpus meum.* In English the translation is "This is my body." In those days only the priests had studied Latin, and only they understood it.

To most people of that time, those initial words became "hocus pocus" and came to symbolize the arcane and secret wonders of religion. As an English word, hocus pocus was first used to describe someone who was a magician, juggler, or of generally questionable character. Now it is used to describe the smoke and mirrors that someone might use to sell their product or idea. It implies that there is very little of substance behind it all.

(It should be noted that some three hundred fifty years later, the Catholic Church decided to celebrate Mass in modern languages, so that there would be less perception of Hocus Pocus surrounding the religion. They did this primarily in response to the success of Protestantism—the competition!)

What does that have to do with us?

I thought you'd never ask.

I was at a trade tasting recently for a group of wines that were all made from the classic Bordelais varieties. As I walked around the room, I could hear the consistent buzz of conversation. These were all wines made from the same kinds of grapes, and each taster was asking the same question of each producer: "What's the blend?"

And each producer, partly out of self-defense, was greeting each taster with a variation of the following phrases: "sixty percent Cabernet sauvignon, thirty percent Merlot, ten percent Cabernet franc." Or "fifty percent Cabernet sauvignon, 50 per cent Merlot." Or "fifty percent Cabernet franc, forty percent Merlot, ten percent Petit Verdot." Or...well, you get the idea. It was one hundred wineries, one thousand tasters, all having the same conversation—a kind of ritual greeting in an arcane language. It was a greeting that was repeated nearly a hundred thousand times at the tasting. All that was missing were the ceremonial robes and the secret handshakes.

With nearly one hundred producers in the room, and a thousand trade guests, the room was humming with interest and excitement. It was, by all standards, a really good event, and a very successful trade tasting. Everyone was delighted with the turnout, and the wines showed very well.

And yet.

I decided to perform a simple little experiment at the end of this tasting. I stood by the door and chatted with members of the trade as they were leaving. I asked them which wines they really liked. Most could name at least one or two producers. And then I asked them the obvious question, "So can you tell me what the blend is for that wine?"

Not a single member of the trade could answer that second question. Not one of them could bring back that information from the flood of rituals that they had celebrated during the tasting. So why were the wineries repeating the information over and over again?

In the end, everyone had a great time, and they felt really good about the tasting. But I am not sure they left fully armed with the kind of powerful information that would allow them to sell more wine the next day.

Which made me think....what was all that conversation about in there? Was it all just hocus pocus?

And that also made me think, "Is that any different from what happens at other tastings?"

I remembered another tasting I attended in New York. I stood at the side of a friend of mine, a handsome young Italian man, as he poured his wines for the tough New York wine trade audience. At one point, a beautiful young wine buyer came by, and he flooded her with information as she tasted his wines. When he was done, he had described each of the vineyards of his winery: the slope, the exposure, the soil type and the yield per hectare. He had carefully explained how each wine is made, carefully handcrafted to capture the essence of its vineyard. And he had provided tasting notes and wine and food pairing suggestions for each of the four wines.

She was obviously enchanted. He was delighted. I was curious.

As she started to walk away from the table, I asked her permission to ask her a question. She agreed, and so I asked her, "What do you remember about what he just told you about his winery and wines?"

She looked stricken, like a deer in the headlights. "Is this a test?" she asked, her voice showing her shock.

"Yes, it is," I replied. "But it's a test for him, not for you."

She thought long and hard about the question, and then replied, "I think he said that his winemaker is a woman."

He had spoken and poured wines for her for nearly ten minutes, and the only thing she could remember about the conversation was that his winemaker was a woman.

I congratulated her on getting the answer right, and then turned to my friend. It was his turn to look stricken. "I am doing everything wrong!" he cried.

Well, not everything. But he had certainly fallen into one of the most common traps in marketing communications. He had spoken about what matters to him, rather than what matters to the target market. And he had wasted a golden opportunity to build a memorable image and marketing message for his brand.

And if you think this is a problem exclusive to the world of artisan food and drink, you've never been to a High-Tech conference!

How many of us do this? Almost everyone. It never fails to amaze me that companies will spend literally hours developing the language they use to describe their products, but will not spend ten minutes with the target market, asking them what they want to know!

The goal of marketing communications is not to communicate what the company knows and does. It is to communicate *what the audience wants to know* about what the company does. And all too often, we talk about our products like scientists in the lab, and not like marketers in the market.

Why do we insist that trade and consumers want to know every single tiny detail in how we grow our olives, harvest our hops, or process our milk? Our competitors want to know this stuff, but they'll never buy our products—they'll ask for them for free.

Perhaps a better idea would be to take a page from the Catholic Church and look at what our competition is doing.

Can anyone tell me the blend in Coca-Cola? Can you tell me how long it spends in the tank, or what kinds of flavorings are added? Can you tell me the source of its ingredients, and what kinds of soil they require?

Nope. In fact, the formula for Coca-Cola is a closely-guarded trade secret, known only to a few top executives at the company. They don't tell anyone, trade or consumer, how the product is made.

And yet they manage to sell a few cases of it here and there—about six trillion servings per year. They don't even explain whether they use wild hops from Canada or olives smuggled into the country from Algeria! How can that be?

Clearly, Coca-Cola doesn't understand what they are doing. If we could teach them a thing or two about selling a product, we could really help their business.

But it is just possible that we could learn a thing or two from them as well. What could we learn?

>> We could learn that if all of us talk about the same things, the message tends to become a hocus pocus of ritual language, meaningless to all but a very few.

>> We could learn that the first lecture in marketing communications talks about developing a unique message that is important and memorable to the target market.

>> We could learn to remember our first MBA lecture, when they told us to come up with the elevator speech and use it every chance we get.

>> We could remember one of the basic laws of advertising, which says that you should talk about benefits, not features.

If you think I'm crazy, I encourage you to visit the website of just about any of your competitors. Look at the home page. Can you tell what the elevator speech for them is? It would seem that the home page of the website is exactly the place to put that speech: those few short words or sentences that really capture what makes them different and unique.

Instead, what you will find is the usual catch phrases, repeated over and over. "We are a small family producer, using only select ingredients, to hand-craft products that taste really good." *Hoc est corpus meum.*

It's a charming message, but it isn't unique or different. And once we get beyond that, just about every artisan producer starts to talk about hocus and pocus.

The worst offenders of all are the product fact sheets. I know, because my company is asked to write these on a weekly basis. And every one of those fact sheets begins with a careful description every single step of the process, from the harvesting of the olives to the aging of the cheese, often with added chemical analyses to give more stuffing to the prose account.

How many of your customers can tell you anything of this information about ANYTHING they eat or drink?

I know the answer to that one, because I ask this question of consumers all the time. The answer is zero. Not one consumer in America today can tell you the pH or TA of any wine they drink. They can't tell you what kinds of hops are in their beer. They might be able to tell you if it's a goat or a cow's milk cheese, but often they can't. And not many of the trade can, either.

Go ahead, ask them.

So why do we include all this information?

I understand the philosophy. (This word, just as an FYI, traces its roots back to the ancient Greek—a love of sophistry, or knowledge!). The philosophy is that everyone else does it, and if we don't we will stick out like a sore thumb.

Now go back and read the first chapter of your Marketing 101 text-book. I think you'll find that it says your goal should be to stand out from the rest of the crowd, so that you avoid being a commodity. You want your brand to stand for something different.

By that measure, at least ONE producer ought to decide to forget the whole fact sheet process, and just tell consumers that their product tastes good, and then talk about more interesting things—like how the world likes to sing in harmony.

(I can hear the screams in the background right now. "But people ASK for this information! We HAVE to give it to them or they won't sell our products!")

I wonder what Coca-Cola says to distributors who won't sell their sodas without knowing the recipe. Surely they have some simple response, like, "How it is made is a secret. People love it. That is not a secret. Now let us show you how you are going to make money selling our product."

Which is, after all, what the trade REALLY wants to know, isn't it?

And our consumers? Do we dare abandon the hocus pocus of blends and barrels, olive cultivars and brewer's yeasts? Do we dare stand out from the crowd?

A few months ago a client told me a wonderful story. She owns the winery and was visiting the tasting room. There the master of the tasting room was expounding, in great detail, on the technical aspects of the vineyards, the wines and the cellar. His target, an earnest young man, was paying rapt attention at every word.

But the other guests in the party were bored—really bored. My client began to chat with the wife of the rapt tasting room visitor…chatting about life, children, and entertaining in her home.

At the end of the visit, the master of the tasting room boasted that he had sold three bottles of wine to the husband. My client then told him that she had just sold three cases to his wife—and she didn't mention barrels once.

I wonder if that changed the approach of the wine geek/tasting room employee? Probably not. It doesn't matter that the consumer doesn't really care, or that the trade can't remember. We will continue on with our methods, sure that we have God and truth on our side. We will continue to offer up the ritual offerings in endless displays of ceremony.

And maybe, after about three hundred and fifty years, we, too, will figure out that maybe we should talk about wine in a language that people can understand, in a way that people appreciate.

We will then really begin to sell our products. And we can forget all this hocus pocus.

CHAPTER 7

THE MATERIALS YOU NEED TO COMMUNICATE WELL: PRESS KIT, PRESS RELEASE, WEBSITES AND MORE

What's A Press Kit?

A press kit is a critical part of your public relations program. It defines the company, provides reference materials to any journalist who is interested, and should serve as the primary source for all messaging and information that comes from your company.

So why are so many press kits so bad?

The first reason they are bad is that the company doesn't want to define itself in terms that really matter. Every artisan producer wants to have a unique story, but most don't have the courage to really step outside the box. As a result, we read the same stories about the same topics: carefully tended vines, handcrafted cheeses, passionate brewers, and true dedication to quality.

The character and identity of your company is blurred by these platitudes, and the remaining point of difference ends up being the personality of the owner. This is all well and good, but I was always taught that the key message had to focus on benefits, not features. What's in it for your customers? How does the personality of the owner of your company affect the flavor of your products? Where is the real benefit to the

---

CONTACT
Paul Wagner, Balzac Communications
707-255-7667, pwagner@balzac.com

For Release 4:00 p.m. P.D.T.: December 4, 2015

Ukrainian Delegation to Harvest the Secrets of the Napa Valley.

Napa, California—On Friday, December 11th, Napa Valley College's Viticulture and Winery Technology Program will host a delegation of fifty MBA students from KMPS, the leading business school in Ukraine, who are visiting Northern California as a part of an international study program to learn from the best in the world. Napa Valley College Winery Program Coordinator, Paul Gospodarczyk, will give the group a tour of the Napa Valley Vintners Teaching Winery, the seven acre vineyard, and Trefethen Lab building at the college, and long-time NVC instructor Paul Wagner of Balzac Communications & Marketing will give a lecture on how the Napa Valley became such a powerful international brand and a world class wine-tourist destination.

"We have an amazing program here," say Gospodarczyk, who also serves as the winemaker at the college's winery "The wines produced here have won major awards at national and international competitions for the last five years in a row." Under the tutelage of a remarkable staff of top Napa Valley wine professionals, Napa Valley College students have gone on to leading positions at prestigious wineries in Napa and the rest of California. "The program attracts students from throughout the United States and around the world," says Gospodarczyk, "and we frequently get inquiries and interest from other regions around the world.'

The Napa Valley College Viticulture and Winery Technology Program is among the largest wine schools in the world, with more than 1,000 students enrolled in three different degree tracks: Viticulture, Enology, and Wine Marketing & Sales. The program's facilities have been supported by many Napa Valley wineries and wine industry suppliers as a conduit by which to inspire and nurture aspiring winemakers. In 2008, the Napa Valley College Teaching Winery became the first bonded winery in the California Community College System. All of the wines produced at the teaching winery are made from grapes that are grown in a seven acre, student farmed, vineyard on the college campus. Every aspect of the winemaking process, from vineyard to bottle, is completed by students on the Napa Valley College campus.

Example of a press release

consumer? If you can't answer that question, then maybe the personality of the owner isn't the key point of differentiation after all.

Do you want an even scarier thought? Maybe you don't have a key point of differentiation.

This is why writing a press kit is such a critical element in the development of a public relations strategy—and why it often takes an inordinate amount of time. The writing isn't hard, but getting the company management to agree on the direction is often almost impossible. All the internal disagreements about direction, focus, and style bubble to the top, and have to be resolved before the kit can be finalized.

Of course, then you have to make sure that it is all true. More than once, we have completed the kit to the exact specifications of the client, only to discover (sometimes months later) that the information we were given was not true. In the worst-case scenario, a friendly journalist tipped us off to the fact that the press kit was not only inaccurate, but intentionally so! That is a nightmare waiting to happen.

Out of fear and trepidation, most companies fail to take important or significant positions. They won't make the necessary policy decisions to really stand out from the crowd. They don't really want to strike off in a new direction, or boldly go where no one has gone before. And the press kit reflects this, from start to finish: Another hand-crafted story about a nice man, woman, or couple who make a nice product just like all the other products on the market.

Wait! You mean yours is different? And yet you can't say how?

If I were a journalist, by the time I had read through about ten of these, I would be plenty tired of the whole idea. And journalists get hundreds of these a year. Your job is to make sure this doesn't happen with your kit.

What Should Go into A Press Kit?

Once you have determined the key messages—the significant points of difference that will really make you stand out from the crowd—you should then support these with a series of reference articles about your company. I have always divided these into two categories: core articles, and peripheral articles.

The core articles are the foundation of the whole kit. A back-grounder should give a complete picture of your company. It should contain and explain the mission statement, trace the history from the beginning to the present day, and introduce the key characters who have influenced that history. This is not an opportunity to "sell" your company as the greatest show on earth—just stick to the facts, ma'am, and let the journalists add the local color. A press kit that is too overtly promotional won't get read; it will get immediately filed in the round file. But it should also clearly state what you think makes you different: your SWOT come to life.

In terms of the text itself, it should be in classic AP style. If you don't know what this means, you shouldn't be writing or editing the press kit. The goal here is to provide the media with the kind of writing that can be adapted for whatever their use might be. If necessary, it should be able to be cut and pasted into an article seamlessly, without suddenly changing voice, style, or perspective. That means writing like a journalist, not a sales manager.

(I am delighted to say that I have seen my writing in *Time, Newsweek, The New York Times* and the *Washington Post*. Admittedly, it wasn't over my byline—but I can show you the press kit or press release where it originated!)

Core articles should also include biographies of each of the key people at the company. How can you tell if you need a bio for someone? If they are important enough that they might get interviewed, then they should have a bio. It should provide a description of what the person actually does, how and where he or she got his/her expertise, and what perspective the person brings to your products. A quote that summarizes how this person views his role in fulfilling the company vision is a good thing to include as well.

Finally, the core articles should include a basic product fact sheet on each product in current release. This is neither a comprehensive analysis of the history of the process, nor is it a sales piece to promote the new discount structure on the whole line. Again, the focus should be the facts. A short note on your specific style for each product is a good place to start, followed by short notes on the raw materials, Mother Nature, and your own process for making it. All of this should fit into two hundred fifty words at most. Keep it short and simple. Then add a short tasting note and any technical data that you feel that you have to include. (Most artisans include way too much technical info. If you make a cheese in the style of a Brie, then just say that, and move on. We don't need to know the temperature of the goat when you milked it. Save that for the technical geeks who specifically ask for this info.)

Please, please provide the suggested retail price. I know—often artisan products will sell for different prices in different markets. But a journalist cannot write about your olive oil without knowing what it will cost their readers, and most know how to adapt the SRP to reflect the actual price in their market. Still don't believe me? Every year I talk to writers who tell me stories about products they love, but won't write about because the company doesn't like to specify prices. If you don't include the price, you are just making it easier for me to get them to write about my clients, instead of your products. Thank you.

(And now, a note about including product samples with a media mailing. Years ago we helped a cheese company launch a new product, and were delighted to learn that the sales team had just closed the deal to stock the product in some important stores in LA. We immediately pitched the story the food editor of the LA *Times*, who loved the story and loved the product. All she needed to go to press was a list of stores where her readers could buy it.

No worries there! We enthusiastically gave her the list that the sales team had given us, and clapped ourselves on the back for a great placement for a great client.

An hour later, the editor called us back. She had called four stores on the list and none of them had the product on the shelves. How could that be? She was furious for having wasted a few hours of her time on a story that she couldn't run.

And we were furious to learn that the sales team had made a presentation to those stores, and the reception was very positive, but in fact, no order had been made or fulfilled.

Moral to that story? Always cross-check an enthusiastic salesperson for accuracy.)

That wraps up the basic press kit. But that doesn't mean your job is over, because part of doing a good job is going beyond the basics. If you have other areas that you think might be of interest, you'd better write up a summary of that information for the press. Free-range Nubian goats? Mountain vineyards? Rare olive trees? Hops from the Island of Doctor Moreau? Barrels formed from the remnants of Tsar Nicholas II's

Press Kit Components
Backgrounder
Biographies of key personnel
Wine fact sheets for each wine
History of the company
Appellation information
Recipes to pair with the wines
Photos to illustrate all of the above
Special interest articles to support the company positioning

sleigh? Write it up and explain, in a simple, factual way, why it matters. You should also consider recipes: how people can enjoy your products in everyday life, along with overviews of unusual styles or techniques you use. Even include special areas of interest in the arts or recreation that you sponsor. And you should have interesting, striking photos to illustrate all of the above.

With these materials on hand, you can now do more than just send out samples. You can pitch story ideas or respond to media requests with the full confidence that when a writer shows interest, you can provide the back-up information they can use to write the story. You have now made good progress from being a PR spieler to becoming a PR professional.

Of course, once you get all of this information together, the sales force will learn about it, and you will then have to produce one thousand copies of the entire kit, so that it can be used at all sales presentations across the country.

Refuse.

A press kit is not a sales kit, and don't ever confuse the two. You should have a different goal for the sales kit, a different budget, and a different method of distribution. They are two different things; don't treat them as if they are the same.

It's true, sales kits should include some of the same information. But the format and use of the kits is completely different, and you should make sure that everyone understands this.

A sales kit should include the hottest reviews for each product, medals and awards and clips from key journalists in major markets. None of these things belong in a press kit. In fact, most journalists resent getting clips from other writers—it seems to imply that they had better write something similar, or else. And even worse, it tells the writer that someone else has already written the story—it's not news, it's not a scoop, and there is no need to tell the story again. Is that the message you want to give the media?

A sales kit should include pricing and profit information. It might also include a color brochure, sales sheets, and order forms. None of this is appropriate to send a journalist. Some of the messages, concerning profits and competitive margins, could actually come back to embarrass you if you send it to someone who writes for consumers.

Salespeople are happy to get information about a company, but it must be information they need, in a format they can use. If they are making twenty sales calls a day, and have to represent a full portfolio of a hundred product lines to each of those customers, they don't have time to read your press kit, and they sure don't have time to talk about it with the customer. Keep your sales messages very focused and simple, without all the backup detail that you provide the press. That helps keep them on message, and allows them to effectively use their time.

I can hear your question even now: "What if the sales people ASK for a press kit? What if they are really interested in our company? Shouldn't we have some press kits already printed so that we can respond to these requests from the field?"

And my answer to you is simple: Who said anything about printing?

I can't remember the last time a writer asked me for a printed press kit. These guys are on deadline. They have limited time and they know how to use a computer. Why would you send them a printed version of anything, when you can send them an e-file that makes their life so much easier? And even more to the point, why would you send them anything, when you can direct them to your website, which should have all of this information right there, in an easy to use and copy MS Word or HTML

Schermeister.com is an excellent example of a simple, clean, and clear website

format? (Not Adobe—it's harder to cut and paste!) Do you want them to use your material or not?

If you want them to use your information, then make it as easy as possible for them to find it. That is what they want, and that is what your competitors are doing. Photos should be at least 300dpi, and recipes should all be carefully tested, proven, and proofed. And you should check how the website works with various browsers, phones, and ISPs, just to make sure that everyone can access it.

(I am always amazed at the number of web service providers who make fun of one or another web browser and refuse to worry about its technology. This is comparable to telling an artisan producer not to worry about the products it might sell in grocery stores, because that's not where the real food freaks shop. Your website should work for everyone, not just the techno-geeks who made it.)

And yes, I said everyone. I have never understood why a company would have a separate section on their website for the press. If you don't want the general public to know about it, why would you provide the information to the media?

Put all of your information, from the basic SWOT message and story to the details about each product, on your website. Make that website easy to use, easy to copy, and easy to navigate. Then tell everyone, not just the media, but consumers, retailer, distributors, restaurateurs—yep, even your own sales team—about it. It is your Bible.

After all, it's a good story, isn't it?

Which brings us to the classic press release. Think of it as a rifle, not a shotgun.

Why do so many people misunderstand the press release? When I talk to media, one of the single biggest complaints I hear about my PR colleagues is that they don't know what a press release is, or when it should be used.

This Isn't Brain Surgery

The real challenge for most of us producing artisan products is that we don't really have any news. And when we do have news, it is frequently of the kind that makes the company want to crawl into a hole and hide, not trumpet it from the top of tall buildings. Nobody would want to publicize the kinds of catastrophic developments that always seem to catch the attention of the news media.

So let's start at the beginning, and see if we can't get all this back on the right track.

What Is News?

This may seem a little obvious, but news is what you see in newspapers, magazines, news shows, and social media sites. If you really want to know what any publication considers to be a good news story, read the publication or watch the other stories that get attention. If you want your story in those media, then you should probably make sure that it fits with the other stories that they run.

The person who decides what goes into a publication or show is called an editor. That person does more than just correct grammar. He or she also decides what the readers or viewers are going to see.

Of course, this particular analytical technique does present some problems. The first problem is that every story you see in the magazine has already been written—and the editor is now looking for something new, not the same old thing. But the flip side of this is that if they have never written a story like yours, chances are they are not going to start with you. Don't waste your time.

For most news media, a news story has to meet some pretty basic criteria.

1. It has to matter to the readership. This is a big challenge for those of us in the artisan food world, because only a small percentage of Americans care about what we do—although that number is constantly rising. It would be far easier to pitch a story about sex or money, because just about everybody cares about sex or money. (I know that we all learned in the film "Sideways" that wine is more important than either sex or money, but until we can convince the rest of the country of this, it's going to be a hard sell. Which means a lot of our stories are destined for geeky publications, at best.)

2. It has to be timely. It has to be new to be news. This is another big challenge for most of us. A good rule of thumb for any press release is simple. As one journalist I know says, "The first thing I ask myself about any press release is: Do I have to write about this today? And if the answer is no, then it goes on the back burner. The back burner is where bad press releases go to die." Most of the stories we pitch in our business are the kind that can wait a few days...or even a few years, to get written.

3. For the best possible results, you should also provide enough background material to put the story in perspective. The fact that you won a gold medal is almost never news. The story that you won the only gold medal at an international competition against more than 10,000 others is a better story. The fact that your product sells for $6, and won against some that sell for more than $600, makes it an even better story. And if yours was made from milk from goats that were raised on the grounds of a brothel in Nevada, it is a slam-dunk. Now you have included both sex and money in the story!

The next time someone at your company asks to see a press release about a new development, put it through that test. Is your new product release something that is of interest to the readers of most magazines? No, it's not—not even of most artisan food or wine magazines. If those magazines wrote stories about every new release or every new label launch there would be no room in them for the real stories they cover.

And, more important, the publications themselves would not get read.

It is always a great learning experience to talk to the people outside of your industry to get their take on this issue. With a few exceptions, they don't care about the kind of endless detail that we often find so fascinating—and they won't read about it, either.

In fact, the best way to learn what the average consumer wants to know is to ask them about their favorites. Ask them what they like about them. Ask them what they know about the company that makes them. You will get anecdotes: stories about people, about friends, and about memorable occasions.

And you want to send out a press release about what?

Press releases are news. The best press releases are about major news: You have just hired Reese Witherspoon to be the chef and culinary consultant; your olive oil has been shown to completely cure cancer. Or, on a less positive note, you are recalling all of your wine because the bottles are radioactive. (See Chapter 14 about that last problem.) Those are real news stories. And they deserve press releases, at the very least.

If you don't have that kind of news, work with your team to make the news you have more interesting. Hire Reese Witherspoon. Cure cancer. Bring into the story the kinds of things that people love reading about: sex and money. No, it isn't easy. But it is what you get paid for. That's how you get attention.

When you do have news, make sure the release follows all of the standard guidelines:

- Your contact information should be at the top of each page. And please make sure that you provide a 24-hour number. Writers hate calling the contact number for information, only to find that they are in voice-mail hell, and can't get the data they need. That release will often go on the back burner...forever.

- The next line should be the timing of the release. If you don't think the timing is important, you don't have news. This also gives journalists a chance to see if the release presents an opportunity for some kind of scoop. If you don't think anyone would be interested in a scoop, you don't have news. Don't send out a release.

- Provide a title that does a good job of summarizing the story—and why it is news. If you can't do this, you don't understand what the media wants in a story, and you are wasting their time. The title is your chance to pitch the release as effectively as possible. If it isn't exciting, why is it news?

- The first paragraph should answer the six honest serving men: what, where, when, why, how, and who. If you don't know all the answers, you haven't done your homework. Writers don't want to wade through pages (or even paragraphs) of information just to find out the basics. Get everything in the first paragraph, and then use the rest of the release to provide additional information and supporting arguments. If you can't really say when it happened, then you don't have news.

- Always double-space the release. True, this is a relic from time gone by, when all releases were printed, and editors liked to write comments on the printed page. But double-spacing makes the document far more readable. That's a good thing.

- Use an easy-to-read typeface. I prefer Times New Roman or Ariel, but keep it simple and easy. Again, if your release needs clever typesetting and graphics, you probably don't have much in the way of real news. And make sure the typeface is at least 10, preferably 12-point type. People have to read this stuff, you know— even old people like me.

- Always provide a few quotes from a key player or two in the story. Journalists often don't have the time to make all the phone calls they would like, and they really appreciate having a few good quotes to use. Please make them sound as if a real person is talking. Market speak about "elevating the benchmark of brand image enhancement" is a sure way to make sure the quote doesn't get used.

- Try to keep each release to one page. If you have to go beyond that, make sure that each page has your contact info, the title of the release, and the page number clearly visible. Things get lost. Your job is to make them easier to find.
- Make sure that you end the release with a # # # or similar symbol. Things get lost. Your job is also to make sure that there is no confusion about what needs to be found.
- Please write in a standard style—AP or New York Times. Journalists are busy. They don't always have the time to re-write every sentence. If your release is written pretty much the way that they would have written it, your chances of seeing it in print go up. If it is written in the style of William Faulkner, it may be much admired, but it won't see the printed page. If you don't know what AP style is, hire someone to write your releases who does.
- And if you are sending this out via e-mail, please don't put it into a PDF. The last thing that journalists want to do is to retype your release word for word. Make it easy for them…and more effective for you. Put it in MSWord or an HTML format.

Once you have real news, and you have finalized that news in a standard press release format, the next step is to get the story out to the media. Not all stories appeal to all writers or even all publications. You must make sure that you have targeted your distribution to the kinds of publications that might actually care about your story.

Wine stories should obviously go to wine writers, wine publications, and perhaps food and lifestyle editors at a variety of publications. But if you really did hire Reese Witherspoon at the winery, then you should also include entertainment writers and editors…and publications that specialize in that field. And the lovely Ms. Witherspoon should be pretty damn near the top of that release.

In fact, we often find that a single press release might get a slightly different treatment depending on where it is going to be sent. If there is a local angle to the story, re-write it for a local or regional publication. Your gold-medal-winning IPA may not be news in Dallas, but it might be in Peoria—if your brewmaster is from Peoria. And the headline for that story is not that your IPA won the gold medal, it is that a local boy from Peoria made a gold medal beer.

This is also true of the kinds of cute, humorous stories we sometimes see in the news. If you are pitching a writer who likes that sort of thing, go get 'em. But if you think that the business editor of a major paper wants to spend time reading about pet koalas and how they got their names, you are wrong. Unless, of course, there is a REAL business story attached, with real dollar figures. I hear countless complaints from journalists about PR campaigns that completely miss the point of their publications. Don't make that mistake, because it makes you look foolish and unprofessional.

One of the most valuable ways to brainstorm any Public Relations campaign is to take a step back and simply imagine the various publications that might be interested in the campaign—if it were presented the right way. Tailor your programs to the media, and tailor individual releases to individual media, and your press clips are guaranteed to improve.

Later we'll talk about getting stories placed in the media without using press releases. That is a whole different ballgame, and requires a whole different approach.

Press Releases You Should Never Write

Deep in your heart of hearts, I know you believe that if the writers and bloggers knew more about your products, your company, your story, or your region, they would write more about you. So you devise a plan to reach out to the media, to stay in contact with them, and to give the reasons to write about you. All well and good.

But as with most things in life, the devil is in the details. The problems begin to arise when you start thinking about what news you have to share. It can get pretty quiet around a conference table when that topic of discussion comes up. It's a bad sign when the product transition charts come out. Yet the marketing team has already decided that it is important to send out a press release a month, even if you don't have news that is worthy of a release.

And more spam is born. I am sure that spam is not the goal of very many PR campaigns, and yet it is the result. Because most companies, whether they are large or small, don't have a good idea of when they should talk, and when they should keep their spam to themselves. Do you want a few examples? Here are some press releases that do a great job of telling the media that you don't have any real news, and so you are going to pester them with spam instead:

By the way, there are worse things than just boring the media with spam. Some press releases can actually offend the media. These are the ones that create such a negative image for you and or your company that they actually damage your chances of future success. The worst ones actually offend the audience they are intended to charm and intrigue. What kinds of releases are actually counterproductive? In my efforts to be helpful, I've even added some suggestions below on just how to do this!

>> "We have just released a new wine. It tastes really good, and here is more technical information than you could ever want on how it was made."

Please. There are 120,000 wines released into the U.S. market every year. If you can't explain why yours is somehow spectacularly different from all the others, then you don't have news. Being one of 120,000 wines is not newsworthy. This is a perfect example of how a winery sees itself in the mirror without understanding the larger market for news. It may be exciting for you and your close relatives, but it is not going to get anyone in the larger market to do anything but yawn. And by the way, your winemaker is not a good judge of what is interesting to the general public.

End result? The media glances at the release, realizes it doesn't have any useful information, and immediately hits the delete button. And the next release you send to them will get less attention. We all receive emails from people we actually like, but never have time to read. Eventually we just learn to delete them without even opening them. The email you just sent to the media is the first step in building this kind of relationship with them.

Do you want to make a release that is counterproductive? Then send out the information about a cheese that has no distribution and is not available in the market. What the heck is a writer supposed to do with this? Write about the cheese, and then explain that since nobody can buy it, it really doesn't matter? I know. You are hoping that the writer will LOVE the cheese, and write about it, and a distributor will see that story, and then call you up and ask to distribute it. And your marketing will be complete!

It doesn't happen that way. Journalists hate writing about products that are not available for sale, because their readers hate reading about them. What good does it do to read about a cheese that nobody can buy? It just frustrates everyone. Every writer knows this. It's about time that you learned it.

Even worse is the press release that not only announces your new olive oil release, but also includes a rave review from another writer. What is the message here? So-and-so loves our olive oil, and you should write about it, because so-and-so is a really good and important writer. This is a slap in the face of the target audience, and will make you many long term enemies if you insist upon it. In fact, there are only a few things that should NEVER go into a press kit that you send to a journalist. One of them is stories by other journalists.

>> "We've just won an award at a beer competition!" We are all
delighted with your success. But try to think this through
from the point of view of the writer. First of all, we know that
there are so many competitions these days that no writer
could ever write about all the beers that won awards. So in the
"remarkable news" category, this release fails.

Who judged this competition? Most beer competitions include a number of writers as judges. For a writer who was not invited to judge this competition, there is likely to be a little resentment. And now you are asking him/her to overcome the resentment and write about the beer? Not likely. And if the writer did judge the competition, this is old news.

There is one kind of release that does merit some consideration under the general topic of competitions. If you have a product that won multiple sweepstakes/platinum/best of class awards, then it might make sense to tie these all together into a release that makes the claim that yours is the most awarded product in its class this year. That would be news, and it just might get printed. But be prepared to defend your position against other companies who might make the same claim.

And if you REALLY want journalists to write about your products, you have to send them samples. Writers simply don't write about products they haven't tasted, so even the very best release will fall short unless you attach it to a sample to taste.

>> "We're hosting a wonderful event that is so special it is by invitation only!" Ouch! Are you trying to offend people? The only ones who will be happy to read this are the ones who are already invited, and they already know about it. Everyone else will have a simple reaction: "Hmmph. They didn't even invite me. What jerks."

Is that really the reaction you want your press releases to achieve? I don't think so. There is no easy way to get around this one. I understand that you are very excited about this event, and are spending a LOT of the marketing budget on it. But you have defined the audience very tightly by your invitation list. And everyone else is NOT INVITED. Don't expect them to write about it. And don't expect them to like or admire you for not inviting them.

Of course, you could open the event up to people who have not received an invitation. You'll need a way to control that, and you will also need a good story to tell the people who were invited. They thought that they were going to an exclusive event, and that event is now open to anyone who makes an effort to show up.

A better solution is to work with a large non-profit with a really good targeted mailing list. You can auction off a few tickets for the event as a fundraiser for the non-profit, and with a little luck you can also get a local society page writer to put in a plug as a way of supporting the non-profit. They won't do it for you or your company. But they might do it to help raise funds for a beloved charity.

>> "Our company is wildly successful. In fact, we have just made a major new investment. But we're a private company, and won't disclose the numbers."

There is a basic rule about business stories: the biggest number wins. If you have a story about a $3 Million deal, and somebody else has a story about a $3 Billion deal, the other story is going to get more coverage. Always. If you refuse to disclose the numbers at all, you are taking yourself completely out of the game. Those are the rules of the game, and you might as well accept them, because they aren't going to change.

I understand that you don't want to display your financial underwear in the media. I hope you understand that the media won't write about people who hide this stuff. Ever.

The solution for this one is pretty obvious. If you want to announce that you are now the #1 selling goat cheese in the world, you are going to have to show some figures to prove it. And be prepared to defend those numbers against both media inquiry and your competitors.

>> "We are now completing the third year of a six year campaign to replant all of our vineyards."

Hard news likes beginnings and endings, not muddy middles. Announcing that you are on-schedule to complete the project two years from now will elicit a wide yawn from most writers. And the other option—that you are way behind schedule, and may not get open in time for harvest—would be an interesting news story. It just won't help the perception of your brand.

If there is something you have completed, then you can announce it. That might get some coverage. Even better, try to find a way that the consumer in the market can experience, for the first time, the results of this big new project. That's absolutely something that could interest a journalist—especially if you allow them a sneak preview of the project and the products. Then they have a scoop, and every journalist likes that!

>> "Pollyanna, who is the cousin of the owner of our tiny little distillery, is going to climb to the highest point in all fifty United States."

In this case, you are confusing your commercial audience with the mailing list for your family holiday newsletter. If Pollyanna doesn't have anything to do with the company, and her adventure isn't part of a larger campaign by the company to help people with disabilities achieve their goals, then this simply is inappropriate for the audience.

Obviously, you could connect Pollyanna's adventure more directly to the company, but beware. The more tenuous the connection to the company and its products, the less likely you are going to get any coverage. And for those really extravagant adventures, make sure that you are not perceived as simply a bunch of silly and rich people playing games while the rest of the country is in a recession. It would be much more interesting to read how your family is helping disabled adults climb stairs than it would be to read about your safari to Africa to shoot animals. Ask King Juan Carlos of Spain—or should I say ex-King?

So what should you write about in your press releases?

Five Keys

>> First, do your homework. Read the writers to find out what kinds of stories they want, and how they want to find them.

>> Make sure that you are promoting something that is of interest to the public, more than something you need to promote to be successful.

>> Ask yourself what the news is. If you can't answer the question, you don't have any news.

>> A good journalist will always ask, "Can this wait for next week?" If your answer is yes, then you don't have news.

>> Make sure you understand the difference between your staff, your distribution network, and the general public. Only write press releases for the general public. The other audience should be contacts with internal communications pieces.

CHAPTER 8

MEDIA TRAINING

Using your spokesperson to tell the story. How to do it well.

As I noted in Chapter Five, one of the top goals of any public relations campaign might be to generate opportunities for you to talk to key media. It's a chance to tell your story to someone who can run with it, get it into print (or on-line) and share it with a much larger audience. It is the single most effective way to distribute your story to the target market.

But there are some risks inherent in meeting with the media. The results are unpredictable, and the power of the media, as an objective third party, can be used to damage your brand as well as polish it. Perhaps most challenging of all, the results of any interview are outside of your control. While we may think that we are charming and clever, the individual journalist with whom we meet may decide something else entirely.

And if that gets into print, it will hurt your brand for a long time to come.

Many times, the pitch bogs down as we begin to see our company owner try to explain the numerous and subtle differences between the blah blah blah.... The writer's eyes glaze over, the owner takes that as complete awe of her expertise, and Houston, we have a problem.

As public relations professionals, we can create a great story, and we can pitch it to just the right audience, but sooner or later, we need to fall back on the company management as the delivery mechanism for the really good parts of the story. And when we do, we often find that they are unprepared, unwilling to learn, and unable to deliver the goods.

They are unprepared because most owners think that they know their story better than anyone else. They may, but they may not be the best people to tell that story. They have all the facts (usually!) but may not know how to edit them, or string them together into a coherent story. And they always run the risk of being perceived as boastful when they get excited.

Journalists often get a little tired of this kind of stuff.

Owner/operators, particularly in the field of artisan foods, are often unwilling to learn because they think they should know everything. Ahem. Talking to the media is a specialized skill, and takes lots of training and lots of practice. It is very different from talking to your employees, customers, or friends. It also has much higher risks.

I cannot stress enough how important it is to have a professional approach to all of this. As an artisan producer, you take great pride in the serious focus you have on your product. You should have the same kind of serious and professional attitude towards your opportunities as a spokesperson for your brand.

I often find that owners don't like to think about this, because they are afraid. They are supposed to know everything about their topic, and sometimes they don't. Who does? Good media training can help them overcome some of this fear, and it can also get them to avoid the simple mistakes we all make when we are a bit nervous and forced to talk to someone who might intimidate us. We don't do our best work.

When I was a very young man, I gave concerts on the guitar. I once gave a concert and noted that a someone sitting in the front row was taking copious notes while I played. I was trembling with fear as I worried what the journalist was writing about my performance, and I am afraid it wasn't my best concert.

Afterwards, that same person came up to speak to me. He was a student of the guitar, and was taking notes on my technique so that he could practice better. Had I known that...

Not everyone is a born performer, and being nervous just makes the situation worse. Only when you are talking to the media, that bad

A Press Tasting

situation can then find its way into print or on-line, to be seen by hundreds, thousands, or even millions of potential customers.

Failure is not an option. Be as professional in your media interaction as you are in the creation of your product. And take as much time to learn the craft.

Make Time for Media Training

The way to avoid this sad scenario is simple. You have to schedule some media training for all the potential spokespeople in your company. That means everyone who might talk to the media, from the marketing manager who meets a journalist at a trade show, to a winemaker who has a winemaker dinner, to the receptionist who answers the phone when the media call. You can't always predict where and when your next media interaction will be, so the secret to success is to make sure that you are prepared for any of the possibilities. I know of one journalist who claims he gets great stories by talking to the spouses of company workers in the supermarket. I bet they don't get media training.

Make sure that you really take the time to do this right. Media training is usually at least a half-day of theory, exercises, and practice. Like
most other things in life, practice makes perfect, so the more time you
devote to practicing this, the better you and your team will be. Practice
in front of different audiences, and in different situations. My favorite
place to practice is in the tasting room, but most top executives won't set
foot in there.

I don't have the space to provide a full-scale media training outline in
this book, but I certainly can give you the basic concepts. This should be
just enough to convince your team that they can do this all on their own...
and well short of what you really need to do this well. Buyer beware!

The first rule of any communications exercise is to understand that
what is communicated depends on two people: the person doing the
talking, and the person doing the listening. We can all listen to a speech
by the President of the United States, but we will each take away different things. Of course, that allows all those media commentators to
make a living following each major presidential speech. The same thing
happens when we talk to the media.

So the first step in any media interaction is to understand what the
writer wants. If you understand what a writer wants, it is a lot easier to
deliver the goods. It is also a lot easier to avoid land mines, if that is the
strategic decision. Sometimes, discretion is absolutely the better part of
valor!

What can be done to maximize your potential for success? Remember my analogy of an interview as a tennis match? Here's how to become
a better player, and to make sure that every shot you hit is the right one.
And remember that your job isn't to win—it's to help the journalist win
in a way that also helps you get your story out. If you think your job is to
win, you are going to lose.

Play The Game for Keeps—Because Every Shot Counts

By the time you are sitting down with the writer, it's too late to ask for
help. You need to be ready to play. In many ways, the first two or three
questions will often determine the whole direction of the interview, and
it is within your power to respond to those questions in a way that will

move things in the right direction. Here are a few tips that you can use to improve your "return of service" for every match.

>> If there is one thing I would stress about being interviewed, it is this: The journalist can choose anything you say as a quote. The interview may last for an hour, but only one or two quotes will make it into the story. And they get to choose which quotes. That is crucial. Make sure that everything you say is a quote you would like to see in print—and I do mean every single thing you say. Every. Single. Thing.

>> Use one of the first questions to let the writer know that you have read a recent article or column, and found it interesting. That shows that you have not only read the writer's work, but also respect the writer's professional expertise.

>> Get your key message out early, and repeat it often. If it is important to you, make sure the journalist knows and understands that. It not only increases your chances that the message will be part of one of your quotes, it will also keep you from talking about other stuff that is off message. You don't want to be quoted off message.

>> If you don't want to answer the question that is asked, answer the question you want to answer. You don't have to answer every question—but when you do answer a question, you have to make sure you really mean what you say.

>> To paraphrase Tommy Lasorda, "Never argue with people who buy ink by the barrel." The writer will always have the last word in print. And you will not. Learn to deflect a delicate question and defuse a controversy without making a permanent enemy who can write about you every week.

>> It's OK to correct something that you said, and the sooner you do that, the better. Don't wait until the next day to call the writer and try to change your story. Take the initiative to say, "I'm sorry, I don't really mean that. Here's what I truly believe."

>> Silence is the most dangerous question of all. Good journalists have learned that if they wait in silence, their interview subject will often continue talking, and say far more than may be

necessary. That's when they get their best quotes. Don't fall for it. Answer the question the way you want to answer it, and then wait, expectantly, for the next serve. The ball is in their court.

So What Do Writers Want?

I break this into two major categories. While every writer should be treated as an individual working on an individual story, understanding these basic categories helps you quickly provide the content and style that the writer wants. Getting that right is what gets you in the paper.

The obvious media contact occurs when we pitch a story to a writer, and want them to write about us. Usually, this is because we have developed a lovely story line, and all we have to do is convince them that it is interesting, and then convince them that it is true. In short, we have a story to sell. But it can also happen at a time of crisis, when we feel it is crucial to get certain facts or information out to the public.

Either way, for us to accomplish our goal, we need the media. And the best way to be successful is to make sure that while we are accomplishing our goal, they get to accomplish one of their goals as well. We have to recognize the goals of the press, and use that knowledge to make our interaction more effective.

The most extreme example of this is when we call the media to correct an error in a story. Our goal is to get our side of the story out clearly and effectively; their goal will be to tell the story as accurately as possible. Approached in that way, both sides can usually come to a pretty quick agreement on a solution. But please bear in mind that accuracy refers to facts, not opinions. Facts are measurable and documented—and can be corrected. Interpretations of those facts, or opinions, are neither measurable nor can they be corroborated by documentation. You won't get a writer to change a story based on those.

Also bear in mind that accuracy is sometimes in the eye of the beholder. Balanced coverage often means that in half of the article you get to tell your story, and half of the time you get attacked!

The other primary kind of media interaction occurs when **a writer calls you** for information on a specific topic. The writer is writing a story, is looking for background data, information about your company or industry, a memorable quote, or specific case histories to illustrate that story. The easy way to respond is to send a press kit.

As you can imagine, I don't approve of the easy way out. Press kits are way too generic for this kind of response, and the writer often doesn't want to wade through pages of biographies and recipes just to get the information he or she needs.

Instead, I will want to talk to the writer, understand what the needs are, and then have my client call back with exactly the information the writer wants. That way we can accomplish a couple of different goals:

> The writer gets the information—and is it accurate and timely.
> We get a quote in the story—because we are providing that personal touch.
> We build a relationship with the writer that bears fruit later on.

Of course, sometimes the media call to get our perspective on something that is a very controversial or negative story for the industry. If there seems to be no benefit to being quoted in this story, refer the journalist to a trade organization that is better suited to handle the situation. And keep your team out of a dirty little fight that doesn't make anyone look good.

Whether we are calling them, or they are calling us, the most critical part of the entire process is the direct, person-to-person interaction with the media. That's where the media training is so critical. To get the most out of such an opportunity, you have to focus your comments so that they make full use of the opportunity. That means being prepared!

Before The Interview

First of all, try to learn in advance what the journalist wants to know, and how it is going to be used. If you can do this, you can tailor your responses much more effectively. While you are at it, try to find out how much the writer already knows about the subject. I once watched a famous winemaker spend twenty minutes explaining the intricate relationship of temperature, SO_2 levels, and the pH levels of wines to malolactic fermentation. The writer then asked what malolactic fermentation was.

Take Four Steps Back, And Start Again!

This is also a good time to decide if you really want to talk to the media about this subject, or if there are any ground rules that you would like to establish. Many of these are implied, but it never hurts to mention them. There are few companies that willingly talk in detail about their competition, and this is a good thing to say up front. And if the writer is insistent about writing an expose story on a really tough issue, you may just choose to be unavailable for that interview. That is part of being prepared.

Preparation of the content is critical, too. Work with a trained professional to prepare your answers to any potential questions, and make sure you prepare for the worst-case scenario. A good interviewer will often start by making small talk to ease the tension, and then slowly tighten the screws to get at the hard topics. Be aware of this, and recognize it when it happens. Nicely and firmly direct the interview back to the subject you had agreed on.

Most importantly, know exactly what you want to say. A good journalist will ask the same question two or three different ways, hoping to get just the right combination of words in the answer. If you have done your homework you will be able to give the same answer three times—in exactly the language you want to see in the story.

This isn't easy. We all naturally try to find new and interesting ways to say the same thing. Some may be clearer than others. Some may sound better, or be more convincing. Every new version gives the media a new chance to quote us. Don't assume that the media will choose the version you like best. They will choose the version they like best. Out of a one hour interview, they will often use only one or two minutes—and they choose which minutes to use.

Practice until you only give your version. Then practice and practice until that sounds perfectly natural.

The Interview

If you read a lot of newspaper stories, and you should, you will see that most of them follow a very specific script. This script is one that we often reject in everyday conversation. When we tell a joke, we leave the punchline for last. Most newspaper stories put the big bang up front, and explain it all further down. It is hard to tell a joke like that, but it is just as hard to get newspaper readers to read four paragraphs of introductory material before they get to the really good stuff.

What does this mean to you? When you are talking to a reporter, tell the good stuff right up front. Focus on your key copy points, lead with your best shot, and then follow-up with the necessary details. For every question, make sure you make room for your key message. That one, off-the-wall comment about strip clubs in Vegas? That is the one quote they will use, every time.

It is important to remember that the media will edit your comments down to one or two good quotes. Make each one of those quotes good. In fact, if you find that one of your answers isn't going the way you want, take the time to stop, ask for a moment, and then correct the answer. And make sure they understand the final answer. This is really your only chance to get it right, so make sure that know when you do.

And don't be afraid to finish what you set out to say. If a reporter loses interest in what you are saying, or tries to push you in another direction, politely but firmly insist that you would like to make sure he/she understands your answer. And then give it again, in its entirety. That is your right as an interview subject.

When you are talking to the media, be open, straightforward, and competent. If you hem and haw, you will give the impression that you don't really know the answer. That is the kiss of death. The way to avoid it? Training and practice.

And while a good writer may ask you to answer a series of hypothetical questions, or to accept a very loaded preface to a question in order to get an emotional response, you should back away politely and take a look at the question coolly and calmly. If you don't like the way it smells, rephrase it in a way that makes you more comfortable. Again, you have that right, and should exercise it.

It takes practice to know how and when to do that. Training and practice.

After The Interview

The first thing you should do after any interview is to replay it in your mind, and identify any problem areas. Did any subject of concern come up? Did you perhaps say something a bit risky, and are not sure that it played well with the writer? Did you miss an opportunity to say something important?

It's not too late. Most writers are more than happy to take a call after an interview, particularly if that call gives them more information or better quotes, or corrects an error they might have made in the story. Think it through, and then make the phone call. Or you can have your agency make the call. Either way, reach out to the journalist, and offer the new material openly and confidently.

You will never get a better chance to correct a bad story than before it is written!

How can you get better at this? Develop your presentation skills.

Who is the best public speaker you have ever heard? Chances are, he or she was not the leading expert in the field. Why? Because presenting information is a combination of knowing the material and reaching the hearts and minds of the audience. That's a special gift, and many top technical experts simply don't have it.

To put it simply, good public speaking is more like theater than anything else. In the end, theater is not about information—it is about performance. For most audiences, it is more important that the speaker be entertaining than truly educational. Would you rather listen to Janet Yellen or Jane Curtin?

From a public relations point of view, we have far more demanding standards for our spokespeople. We need them to capture and hold the attention of the audience, and we need them to convince even the most skeptical of critics. In addition, we ask them to be effective at everything from a full-blown presentation at a large conference, to a one-on-one meeting with a single journalist.

That is a tall order for any spokesperson. The irony is that most of our company spokespeople are not chosen for their skills in this area; they are chosen because they are owners, or managers. While making a great product may be as difficult as assuaging the concerns of a critical journalist, the skills involved are VERY different!

I am not suggesting that you need to hire one of Hollywood's leading actors to play the role of your spokesperson. I am suggesting that being a company spokesperson is not something that comes naturally, and the role requires both training and practice. While many people do have natural communications skills, all of us can improve upon these skills to make the most of every media or public relations opportunity.

The Medium vs. The Message

Yes, I know what Marshall McLuhan said, but in the public relations field, most of the time the message is more important than the medium. In fact, most good public relations professionals spend a lot of time making sure that the message for their client is consistent and clear, throughout all of the various applications and media.

In this book I have spent a large amount of time on the importance of focusing your energy on a few, very clearly defined messages: messages that will define your brand positioning and clarify your unique selling proposition. If you don't have those messages burned into your brain, then stop here. Do not pass Go. Do not collect two hundred dollars. And for goodness' sake don't talk to the media! Talking to the media when you don't know what you want to say is the perfect way to put yourself into a position that will take many years and many dollars to escape.

If you DO have those messages clear in your mind, then spend some time with your team refining the language. Most companies don't spend enough time making sure their messages are clear to the appropriate audience. My favorite rule about this sort of thing is that the messages you develop should be clear and concise enough that a well-educated twelve-year-old can understand them.

No, I am not advocating marketing wine or beer to minors. I am stressing that many artisan messages get so complicated, and involved such a technical knowledge of the industry, that most consumers, and many in the trade, are lost. Or even worse, they are bored.

I was recently asked to give a speech at a marketing conference in Italy, and was fascinated by some of the other presentations. In the land of Sophia Loren and Marcello Mastroianni, of *Under the Tuscan Sun* and *Tales of the Decameron*, of da Vinci and Prada, the focus was on tiny nuances of soil and climate, extensive explorations of pH levels and micro-oxygenation. I was appalled.

I suggested that the message had become completely transformed into a parody. As an example, I asked the audience to join me in meeting a beautiful woman, or an attractive man. Then I asked the audience if they wanted to know about the chemical make-up of these beautiful bodies. Of course they didn't. Who cares if they were composed of thirty-five liters of water, and twenty kilos of carbon? The audience wanted to fall in love, not perform a gas chromatography analysis.

Your spokesperson will be much more successful if you keep this in mind. Yes, every artisan product comes with long list of fascinating production techniques. At least they are fascinating to other producers and academics. But what most people really want to know is what makes you different. That usually cannot be answered in terms of chemicals or processes. What makes you different is the vision you have—the dream that created your product. We dream about the things we love: people, places, and passion. Put your message in those terms, and you will reach into your audience's hearts.

Play It Again, Sam

Once you have that message, and you are sure that it is working well, the next job is to deliver it over and over again. My experience in this business shows that it takes two or three years for such a message to begin to work its way through the market pipeline. While it may be appealing to change your message every few years, it is more likely that consumers and the trade are confused by this, rather than convinced by it. Stick with the program, and stay on course.

This is not just a general rule for long term strategic planning. It is also an excellent rule for every interaction, every presentation by your spokesperson. Whether it be an interview with a journalist, a presentation to a small group of retailers, or a large scale speech to consumers, your job is always the same: to make sure that they understand completely and perfectly the message of your company, products or brand.

In a prepared speech, this is relatively easy, as the language can be crafted in advance, and the message carefully stated and re-stated as often as necessary. You should never have any doubt that the audience understands your message in such a venue.

In less formal settings, this focus becomes the job of the spokesperson. Each question should be addressed from a single point of view: How can this question be used as a platform from which I can deliver my message? Each requested quote should get that same careful analysis. Effective politicians have taken this to a fine art, when every question is simply an excuse for them to give one of five simple "sound bites" that they have decided will determine the next election.

This may sound callous and philistine, but the reason they do this is simple: It works. It gets them elected, and usually keeps them out of trouble. And those are admirable goals for any communication program!

Does this mean that you have to be a mindless zombie, repeating catch phrases ad nauseum? No. But it does mean that you should be very clear about your goals in a speaking environment, and you should make darn sure that you are not flying blindly into uncharted territory in a way that will come back to haunt you for years into the future. Unless you are as gifted as Robin Williams, that usually means sticking to the script.

Words Alone Are Not Enough

In every interview or presentation, there is always the possibility that the listener will misunderstand something that has been said. Most times this is quite innocent, and can be cleared up with a simple question or two. But for a very tough, critical audience, or an interviewer with a grudge, this can create the opportunity for some real problems.

One of the solutions here is to make sure that your listeners know what is important. How do good speakers indicate that? First of all, they will say it in so many words. They will use phrases such as "This is the most important thing about our company," or "If there is one thing that you remember from my talk today, it is this…"

Of course, repetition can achieve some of the same goals, as can adding emphasis to a point by increasing the volume of your voice, or accentuating your hand movements. (Those of a certain generation may even remember Nikita Khrushchev pounding on the table in the UN with his shoe!) In smaller groups, making an effort to make eye contact during key points is also a good way of emphasizing a key point. Only use the shoe tactic when speaking at the UN.

It should go without saying that if you don't believe something to be true, then you shouldn't say it. You are far better off admitting that some of your past releases have not lived up to your expectations, than you are insisting that every wine you have ever made was great. The first option gains you credibility and respect from the audience. The second simply makes you seem arrogant and shortsighted. Which would you rather achieve?

Looking your audience right in the eye is always a good technique, because it also allows to you get a certain amount of feedback from their reactions. The telltale signs of averted eyes, coughing, fiddling with papers, or getting up and leaving the room are all indications that you are not reaching the audience where they live...and they are letting you know about it. When that happens, it is time to draw things to a close, or take a dramatic step to win back their attention. Take off your right shoe....

And finally, in any public situation, it is usually a very bad idea to talk about other producers or other brands. Speak about your vision, your dreams, and your successes, but don't try to make yourself a critic of the industry at large. Save that for the men and women of the press— who don't have to sell anything next week!

The Bigger the Group, the Larger the Gestures

When you are speaking to a very large group, be aware that you will need to change your performance to be effective. This is why some actors are better on screen, others on the stage. These days, with the huge video screens of some conference facilities, this is less of an issue, but I still believe that bigger is better when it comes to presentations to large audiences.

The first step is to get their attention, right at the start. This is why most speakers begin with a joke, a technique that works well if you know how to tell a joke. If not, stick to the script, but lead with the exciting stuff up front. Don't save your best line for last, because by that time, many of the audience will already be reading their phones in their laps.

If you want the presentation to be interactive, then make it that way from the beginning. Don't speak for fifteen minutes without interruption and then ask the audience to get involved. They will already have sat still so long that they won't be able to move. Start things with a poll, ask them a controversial question, or get a few people to offer an opinion. The rest of the crowd will automatically get more involved right away.

It is important to remember that every single person in that audience is pulling for you. None of them wants to sit through a tedious presentation, so they will absolutely give you their best shot at being a good audience. If you treat them well, they will repay that effort with sincere gratitude. Establish a common ground from which you can begin your journey, and give them a very focused and hard-hitting presentation. As you have heard so many times, introduce your concepts, present them, and then summarize them again.

How long should you talk? Less than you think. Don't be afraid to end early—no speaker was ever booed for not using every minute allotted to him or her. But plenty of speakers have ruined a good presentation by going into more detail, and greater length that the audience wanted. Remember that excellent advice from the theater: Always leave them asking for more.

Smaller Groups Mean More Listening

Many of the techniques presented above work well for smaller groups as well, but there is one key element that is different: In a smaller group, it is much easier to read the audience, and work with their reactions.

Here eye contact is even more critical, because one or two lost lambs can stampede the whole situation. And the interactive presentation is actually much riskier here, as the rigid format of a large group will not protect you quite so much. Be careful how you do this, and make sure that you are reading the room dynamics correctly.

With a smaller group, it is easier to determine who is the key listener, and play to him or her more directly. When you speak to individuals, use names if you can, and take the time to respond to people directly, rather than in general. It is your job to keep the ball moving, so please don't sit back and watch some of the audience take over the show. It will be hard to take control again without a lot of effort and a lot of help.

It's Show Time!

I like to think of every presentation, every interview as a piece of theater. Some performances are in opera houses, and others are small set pieces in a drawing room. Still others can be as intense and focused as "Waiting for Godot." In every case, you need to understand who the audience is and what they want. You have to understand your role in the production perfectly, and that of the other actors. And then you have to make it work.

You won't get a standing ovation very often, but you may get to be pretty good at delivering your messages to key audiences in a way that is both effective and memorable. In my book, that is success.

Key Points:

Know your message backwards and forwards.
Believe your message with all your heart.
Deliver that message without getting distracted by sub-plots or diversions.
Don't just repeat yourself, reach out to the audience.
Relax and have fun.

CHAPTER 9

SOCIAL MEDIA AND RELATIONSHIP MARKETING

If you think that the internet is the latest in high tech communication, you are two or three generations behind the constantly expanding envelope of communications technology. And to hear some people tell it, you should be spending most of your time chasing these various new applications so that you don't get left so far behind that nobody even notices you're gone. To hear my children talk about it, I am already well past the point of no return.

Well, yes and no.

Newspapers, and almost all printed media, are in a world of hurt. And if you want to really get excited about something, get excited about the number of really good journalists who have lost their regular voice in a printed publication over the past year. True, almost all of them now have blogs, where they have more freedom to write what they want, but a blog is not the front of the lifestyle section for *USA Today*.

However, the print media is fighting its own battles, and I am not sure that a book like this will turn the tide one way or the other. In short, I have come not to praise print media, but to bury it—or at least offer an alternative solution.

The Alternative to Print

What new alternative is replacing these venerable publications? It's a blend of Web-based social media: Blogs, Facebook, Twitter, YouTube, and a host of others that have found a new and vibrant audience without printing a single word on dead trees. (See? Even old dogs can learn a few new tricks!)

No matter what happens to print media, the future, sooner or later, is the internet, and instead of complaining about it, you really should start to figure out how to play the new game. Because in just a few years, nobody will care about the games you currently know how to play. As proof of this pudding, I cannot count the number of print journalists who have called me in the last couple of years, exploring career alternatives. If they are getting the message, so should we.

It is equally important for you to understand who is playing these games, and how to win. The demographics of these new applications are much younger than the usual demographics of the wine industry, but that is no reason to walk away. In fact, these younger consumers are a bright shining generation of new consumers who are bursting on the scene and creating enormous growth in sales of all kinds of artisan food and drink products. They are experimental, adventuresome, fearless, and willing to buy good-tasting, good-for-you, products. And they are more at home on the Web than they are thumbing through the pages of print media.

The Outreach Programs

Let's take a look at some of the applications here, and see what works and what doesn't work for companies who want to reach consumers and the trade with their stories. Let's start with a blog. This is a kind of on-line diary that allows you to write whatever you want. It also can be structured so that only certain users can access it, although I am not exactly sure why a consumer company would want to limit access.

Should you have one? Maybe. But if you think a blog is the internet version of the usual company newsletter, then you need to go back to square one and start again. Blogs should be fun, informal, and personal. What attracts readers in a blog is not the official statement of the vice-president of marketing, but a funny and cute anecdote about the family dog. Blogs can create a real sense of personality about a brand, and can engage consumers and the trade on a very emotional level. But to do that, you have to be willing to take chances and let your underwear show a little bit.

Approach this the same way you would approach a traditional journalist. When you read the publication, you get a solid idea of what kinds of stories are of interest to the journalist. When you read the successful blogs, you will see what works and what doesn't work. And please don't think that you can change this blogosphere world. This is a young audience, and they want fun and entertainment. They don't want the introductory course of a local university program as your blog. If you can't write this stuff, or find someone who can write this stuff, you are better off without a blog. Seriously.

On the other hand, if you have a bright young tasting room employee who has a knack with language and can be trusted to tell some fun stories about her experiences in the tasting room, you just might have the beginnings of a successful blog.

If you do follow that path, bear in mind that your blogger will assume the personality of the company for many consumers. Be careful that you choose wisely and well—and that you review and edit every post to make sure it is consistent with the messaging you want to present.

If the written word isn't enough, you can always follow the same path with your own, home-made videos. No, you don't need a production crew: sometimes all you need is a nice cell phone with video capability. That's enough to post something on YouTube.

YouTube is one of the most remarkable developments in the decade. If you have ever wondered about any story, legend, silly trick or bizarre and exotic behavior, there is a video about it on YouTube. It is quite possible to spend hours just following one thread into another, from magic tricks to archery tricks to medieval archery to medieval medicine to... well, you get the idea. And it is all on video, so you can watch it again and again.

How can you use YouTube to generate success? Again, by watching what is successful and following along in the same vein. Ohio Wines and Producers has a project that starts with a pair of engaging young women who visit each winery on the trail and produce a short YouTube video on that winery and its tasting room. It's a great idea, and should generate a lot of interest. Each of the wineries has a special focus, and the two women are not Masters of Wine, but simply fun and engaging young people who are enthusiastic about what they are seeing and doing. That's a good recipe for success on YouTube.

At the same time, a video of your winemaker tasting through twelve vintages of Cabernet in a vertical tasting won't generate a lot of interest, unless he manages to mimic Lucille Ball and slowly degenerate into inebriation over the course of the tasting. Nor will an endless video of milk curdling. What works here is fun, approachability, and an occasional gaffe. If you want everything you produce to be perfect, you won't get a lot of attention on YouTube.

**Big Table Farm does great social media marketing
via Instagram**

Unless, of course, the cameraman manages to keep a bunch of the out-takes from the project and create a montage of them. That will get you lots of attention!

I can hear you now. This is all pretty scary. Most companies won't host a forum or message board because they are afraid that someone will write something critical about them. And these new social media are a lot more dangerous than that. In fact, there is a well-documented example of an airline that lost about forty percent of its bookings in a couple of weeks after a social-networked young consumer starting posting the story of his grievances on line. Ignore these at your own peril!

As I have always counseled my clients: When a journalist calls, you don't have to talk to him. The thing to remember is that the journalist is going to write the story anyway, so you might as well give your input into the story. The same is true of these new media. They are going to notice you, sooner or later. And unless you are paying attention, you will likely be blindsided by it all.

Who's Talking—And How to Respond

One way to avoid this is via an on-line search engine that follows key words for you. If your name is cropping up on the internet, wouldn't you like to know how and why? Google has a search program that will allow you to get a heads-up on what's being posted about you, and where. You should do that at least once a week, if only to make sure that there isn't a firestorm around the corner. I consider that part of basic due diligence. But once you start finding your name on the web, you will still have to master the rest of these social media applications to respond with any success.

Facebook might be a good place to start any real response. It's a great way to build community around a brand. You should have a goal of transforming some of its customers into ambassadors—missionaries who travel the land spreading the good word about the brand. Facebook is a great way to make this effective. You can add each of those ambassadors as your friends, and give them the tools they need to tell the story about your company and your product. It's a fun, interactive tool to build a family around.

It's also very easy. I think I set up my Facebook page in less than three minutes. Of course, mine didn't have to be approved by the vice-president of the company or the corporate attorneys. Why aren't you doing that already?

I haven't mentioned a company webpage here, simply because I assume you already have one, and it is working for you. If that is not true, please go out and hire someone under forty as your marketing manager, and get to work!

A more complicated question is Twitter. This very active application allows members to send very short (and usually grammatically amputated) messages like wildfire to a pre-selected list of their friends, homies, or peeps. (Don't have peeps? Get some!)

But Twitter has limited applications for commercial entities. Much of the Tweeting is somewhat mindless notes about menial tasks and the day-to-day minutiae of the posters: hardly the stuff of success. I tend to think of Twitter the way I think of a press release—it's a waste of time if you don't have good information. If you have no news, there is no point telling people about it.

But let's go back to that vast army of ambassadors that you have created for your brand. As they sit at their computers or talk on their cell phones all day, you can use Twitter to reward them for being friends of your products. When you get a double-gold medal at the Monterey International Competition, why not set up a Twitter account that allows you to spread the word to your closest friends? Better yet, why not include an offer for them to buy some of the award-winning product at a slight discount, before the rest is all sold out in a massive block to your biggest distributor? Twitter may not be the best way to keep on on-line diary of your day, but it is a great way to let your key customers know about special offers or sweet deals.

Are there others? Of course. Linked-In gives you a great way to build relationships in our commercial fields in a professional way. These might be great tools with which to build a network for your distributor salespeople...and your contacts in the industry for when you lose your job, or they lose theirs.

Are you still keeping business cards on file? These programs make business cards obsolete.

Jumping the Shark?

Sorry, I couldn't resist using a catch phrase of these new media, and nothing will make the point more effectively. Because by the time you read these words, that phrase will already be old hat, and NOBODY who matters will be using it.

(To jump the shark means that users have tried it, used it, and are now jumping to new/different/possibly better applications. And it is no longer in common use because people have, in fact, jumped the shark on it.)

With that in mind, don't invest too much in these applications without understanding two key facts:

1. Whatever is hot today, there is every likelihood that it will be passé in a few years. Don't count on anything being constant in this world, except change. That's not a reason to avoid them—you can't afford to do that. But it is a reason to follow them and stay involved. Listen to your customers, and communicate with them via the methods THEY prefer. That's not revolutionary technology; that's Marketing 101, and has been true since the day the first amphora of olive oil was sold in the first market in ancient Sumer.

2. They will take up a huge amount of time. As a small company, you don't have a lot of money, so your only other option is to invest time. But it is important that you invest it wisely, and don't think that writing an entry blog once a month is going to change your sales and marketing plan. It won't. It will only make you look old and out of date—and make you frustrated as well. But I will bet that your tasting room staff has time, early in the morning, before they get busy, to reach out to customers via these new social media. And if you can't trust them to do this stuff, why have you hired them? They are speaking to your customers every day!

Keys to New Media

1. Get involved, because the world is passing you by.
2. Look before you leap—learn the system and the social rules before you dive in.

3. Invest time and energy into these, because they will help you reach your market.

4. Be prepared to change as the market changes technology and applications.

How Different Is the New Media?

We're all being assaulted with the news that we are out of date, out of touch, and being left far behind by a generation of e-savvy consumers who are born, live, and die on the Web without ever making contact with another individual. And they ARE the future.

So what can we do to reach these strange beings? And what do we need to do differently?

The answers are both comforting and quite terrifying. In terms of content, some of us are already doing all the right things. If the brands we represent are well defined, and the brand identities have real personality and positioning, then the marketing communications content should be pretty good, no matter who the audience is.

But the delivery system? Ah. That's another matter entirely.

Websites:

By now, just about every company on the face of the planet should have its own website. After all, since most teenagers have their own space, it only makes sense that you have one as well.

On a basic level, your website should combine the functions of a number of standard public relations publications: the brochure, the press kit, the distributor sales kit, a newsletter, and a tasting room sales piece. It should all be on one site, and it should be fully up to date. It is simply the easiest and best way to communicate the most information to the widest range of audiences completely and effectively.

Just to give you an idea of how completely I believe this, Balzac doesn't have a single printed marketing piece: no brochure, no folders, no paper at all. Everything we do is on the Web.

After all, one of the huge advantages of a website is that it doesn't have to be re-printed every time you release a new product, hire a new brewmaster, or change your label. That's a very good thing—but only if you make sure it is up to date. Often, the website lags far behind reality. There is no excuse for this. Take all of that money that you had budgeted for print jobs over the next three years, and put it into making your website really informative and really effective.

When it comes to your distributor and sales network, you need the very latest information at every level, from hot reviews and product tech sheets to current graphics and data. If you don't have someone updating your website every week, you are missing the boat on this one. That great review isn't going to be nearly as impressive when it is six months old. Get it on the Web twenty-four hours after it comes out. We use a Web clipping service as well, so that we can sometimes get the stories almost before they are printed.

How many artisan companies include short ten- and twenty-five-word menu descriptions on their websites? Very few, and yet this is one of the most often requested services from on-premise customers. If you put them on the website, you'll limit the number of after-hour emergency calls from your sales team.

What makes a website effective? Despite what many designers and video gamers say, the best way to make a website good is to make it simple and informative. Get the information on the page, and make it easy to find. We have all had the experience of waiting for a large and very complicated website to load—and we have all clicked away before the Intro began to play. Keep that in mind. Your spectacular Intro page may just be someone else's slow road to oblivion. If they don't see it, it doesn't matter how really wonderful it is.

If there is one mistake that many web professionals make, it is that they overestimate the connection speed of the American consumer. Save the flaming baloney and large images for techno-geeks. Your job is to get the message across using good, simple graphic design and good marketing strategy. Special effects are what designers use when they don't understand marketing and strategy.

Your website should completely convey the image and marketing message of your brand, and it should do so very quickly. If your website can be confused with any number of other websites, with beautiful pictures of vineyards, still-life photos, and photos of happy family members, it's time to re-think the whole thing.

This isn't a family holiday card, it's a marketing and sales piece!

Speaking of selling your product, that's another key role for your website. There isn't space enough here to get into that subject, but it's something that you should learn and understand if you want to be successful.

What I do want to mention is the role that websites must play in relationship marketing. Since most artisan producers are too small to do true brand marketing on a national basis, relationship marketing must be the solution. And on the Web, relationships mean real people. You have to participate. You have to answer questions, write personal notes, and treat the people visiting your website very much the way you would treat someone visiting your tasting room or your table at an event.

Have you ever been to tasting where a producer simply set up a poster of the product label and left the product on the table for people to serve themselves? It's a disaster. So is a website that doesn't answer its email, or respond to customers with a live personality.

It's all a part of building a community of relationships around your company. Whether the people are on their phones, or attending a tasting, you want to make personal contact with them. And you want your best people to be the ones who make contact. In my experience, IT departments are not the best people to build personal relationships with your customers. They are too busy building personal relationships with your computer system!

There is no difference between a promotional dinner, a tasting in New York, or an email inquiry to your company. All of them are opportunities to build the network of family and friends around your products and company. If you understand that, you will have a much better chance of success. Those who don't understand it will fail.

I'll make one final note about websites. We once had the opportunity to test whether consumers would prefer to send their questions to a live expert sommelier, or a cartoon character who promised to answer them. The cartoon character won, five to one. When it comes to expert questions, consumers are still intimidated by the experts, and anything you can do to ease that pain will reap big rewards.

Beyond your own backyard:

Blogs from traditional media

Lots of print publications now have blogs from many of their journalists. These are a somewhat less formal kind of reporting, and they allow the reporter to add depth to a story, or give a personal shading to a story that might need more explanation. Because these are less formal, they usually have less impact in the marketplace. But they are still in writing, they can still be quoted, and they still matter. These blogs are just another reason to treat all of the media with professionalism and focus.

The easiest way to develop relationships with these bloggers is to do good, professional PR work with them and their publications. What doesn't pay off in print coverage may still find a place in the blog-work of the same journalists.

There is one advantage of a blog, which is the advantage of all e-media. If there is a factual error, they can and should be corrected as soon as possible, before they become part of a larger viral infection of quotes and citations.

Blogs From New Bloggers

But there is a much larger category of bloggers in cyberspace. They are often young, and often not affiliated with print publications. These are the bloggers who have no credibility other than what they can create by what they write. They are not endorsed by any larger authority, other than their own audience. Are they experts? Are they fair? Do they follow the standard procedures and ethics of journalism? Who knows? But some of them have developed quite a following. And if they can deliver a message to an audience, they are someone we have to take seriously.

We often approach these bloggers the way we would approach any young journalists. They may not have the authority and power of some of their older colleagues yet, but some of them will. And we can't always tell which ones will reach that level. We try to develop relationships with anyone who writes about our clients. That means sending them information, inviting them to events, and providing occasional samples for columns.

It also means learning as much as we can about them. We always try to tailor our efforts with the media, and bloggers are no different. If we find someone who is really interested in a product we represent, and they can help us get our message out to a good audience, we will work like heck to make that happen.

Will all of these bloggers gain the audience and power that will make them a force in the your industry? No, they won't. But these days, when a young journalist may even use his or her blog instead of a resume to find a different job, it pays to work with them to make their writing as effective, true, and informative as possible.

Like some writers who have produced newsletters that flowered and then died, some of these blogs will die as well. But others will grow, and that growth will be based on style, credibility, information, and energy. Where we can help that happen, we should do so.

Chat Boards and Forums

At many of the top artisan food and beverage websites, there is a specialized audience of chat boards and forums. These are opportunities for anyone in cyberspace to participate in discussions, share their knowledge and emotions, and feel part of the larger community of the website. There are relatively few rules, and the content reflects that.

Beware: If you ever want to lose faith in the future of our world, visit one of these sites during a vicious flame war about some topic of current interest. You will become convinced that it is all about ego and vitriol, not joy and appreciation. Joining in one of these discussions can feel very much like walking out onto a tightrope with your pants around your ankles.

On the other hand, behind the cyberspace intimidation, many of the participants in these chat boards are gatekeepers or influencers with key roles in our artisan world. And the opinions they express are real. These boards are a great tool to find out what some of these people are thinking, and a great way to get a sense of some of the rumor mills that generate buzz in the industry. We think it is very important to monitor what is being said.

But we proceed with caution in terms of participation on these boards. It is important to correct misinformation that is cited, but be prepared to document what you say, and defend your role in the discussion. Be up-front about any affiliations you may have with the brands, companies, or causes that are being discussed. Be respectful, honest, and factual in your posts. If you do all of that, you can still expect at least some of these people to flame you in unattractive ways. But by building personal relationships with them, you will accomplish something. It is always easier to write something really critical if you have never met the person, either live or on-line. Building these relationships does introduce a level of courtesy and consideration. That can be really important in the cyber-world.

DIY Chat Boards and Blogs

Of course, you can always decide to host your own chat boards, and post your own blogs as a way of creating a sense of personality and community around your products or brand. If you do so, I would suggest that you keep a couple of key factors in mind. What most of your visitors want is a peek behind the scenes. They want to be included in a special group of family and friends who know a little more about your company and the people behind it.

This does not mean more in-depth details about your production techniques! It means that they want the kinds of stories they can tell around a dinner table about the company and its people. They want intimate looks, not detailed technical information. If you don't know the difference between these two things, get someone else to run the blog.

Chat boards hosted by companies are dangerous, simply because they can offer cybernuts the opportunity to attack your products, service, and integrity on your own home turf. Don't even consider hosting one of these unless you plan to have someone monitor it every couple of hours. And if you insist that the topics be very focused on you and be very complimentary to your products, you will find that you have an audience of about three people, one of whom will be your mom—if she knows how to participate in a chat board!

On the other hand, these boards can be wonderful ways for your customers to share stories and experiences, coordinate a group adventure to your tasting room, and give you feedback on everything from your new label to the winemaker dinner in their home town. I think the rewards are greater than the risks, but I am very comfortable in cyberspace.

If you want to take this technology to the next level, you can have your winemaker do video tasting notes on all of your wines on YouTube videos, complete with an amusing outtake that makes him look just a little more human and likable than usual. You can organize podcasts of the olive harvest or a cooking session with a top chef using your cheese. You can invite media to join you for an on-line tasting of your best products, complete with a video feed.

It's all possible. Other companies are doing these things successfully. They are your competitors. How are your products selling today? How will they sell to the next generation?

Keys to Success

1. Create and maintain your website as if your business depended on it. It does.
2. Treat all journalists professionally, whether they are on-line, on-air, or in print.
3. Join the e-community and learn to play that game.
4. Participate personally in the communication, if you want to build relationships with your target market.
5. Don't stop here—you're already five years behind the curve.

Case Study:

There are few wine regions in the world that have a more traditional image than Bordeaux. The classic stories of chateaux, elegance and heritage have often made these wines intimidating to the average young consumer. In this evolving market, the Syndicat des Bordeaux et Bordeaux Supérieur wanted to reach out to these new consumers, and increase their reach in the American market.

The key was to update not only the message, but also the medium for the messaging about these wines. The less expensive and more approachable wines of Bordeaux and Bordeaux Supérieur are an ideal introduction to the world of Bordeaux, but to reach these new consumers, we needed to focus our efforts on conveying a fresher, more vibrant image of the wines and the region.

In terms of the messaging, it was critical to give more information on the way these wines are used every day in Bordeaux, and we did this with personal stories about the Bordeaux lifestyle and the next generation of Bordeaux winemakers. These winemakers are lively, energetic and fun...exactly the right people to change the staid image of more traditional Bordeaux.

But we also realized that approaching the same traditional wine journalists and critics who have written the same stories about Bordeaux year after year would not get us the results we wanted. More and more consumers (especially our target of Gen Xers and Millennials) are choosing to receive their news and information not from newspapers and magazines, but online from less traditional websites and bloggers. We needed to reach this younger and more open audience, and so we needed to work with these new media.

Along with a new interactive website and blog, we began to utilize social media tools (Facebook, Twitter, etc.) to promote the wines of Planet Bordeaux, the U.S. marketing program established to promote the wines of Bordeaux and Bordeaux Supérieur. One project in particular was a rousing success.

Working with a group of winemakers in Bordeaux and our Bordeaux-based counterparts at Vin'Animus, we put together a live virtual tasting using the Twitter network. This involved reaching out to a national list of non-traditional media, such as wine bloggers and those who write for electronic media such as Examiner.com, and inviting them to participate in a simultaneous tasting of the wines on-line. Expecting a handful of participants, we were delighted that our outreach generated an overwhelmingly positive response. We received requests from thirty-five different wine media and bloggers to participate in this event. We shipped wine samples to each participant in advance of the tasting, and provided them with information and contact numbers so they could follow along as we tasted the wines, live, with a live Twitter feed for all the participants.

The day of the tasting, a Balzac account executive along with participating producers in Bordeaux acted as hosts for the tasting, and each of the wines was tasted one by one. The media participants tasted the wines, posted comments on their impressions and asked questions of the producers in real time. The producers were focused on answering the specific questions about the wines, and our Balzac team focused on keeping the conversation moving in the right direction.

In the end, the back and forth communication became an invigorating exercise in controlled chaos. Questions, answers, comments, and jokes all flew around the internet, and for roughly two hours the wines of Bordeaux and Bordeaux Supérieur were the talk of the Twitter nation. Because of our flexibility and enthusiasm, the event created a very positive image of a modern style of Bordeaux wines and Bordeaux winemakers, and many of the participants expressed how much they enjoyed the wines and the experience.

In the end, the media results were quite impressive. Not only did the thirty-five bloggers participate, but we had an additional forty-nine consumer "tweeters" join in the conversation. Although they had not received the wines, they were active participants in the conversation, and added to the excitement. This clearly indicated that there was definite interest for the wines and that we generated some positive buzz within our target market.

In total we generated 1,088 "tweets" during the tasting, exceeding more than all previous tweets about Planet Bordeaux combined. Those tweets reached a potential audience of 184,052 people with 2,497,312 total impressions. And finally, in a more traditional method of measurement, more than fifteen of the media and blogger participants wrote about the event and the wines on their blogs.

In a two-hour time window, we were able to generate more buzz for Planet Bordeaux than ever before. The success of this event, and the buzz generated, allowed us to leverage that momentum in future communications with the participants and other non-traditional media.

A few years later, we executed a similar program for a major Napa Valley winery in more than seventy TotalWine stores nationwide. The numbers were off the charts.

CHAPTER 10

SPECIAL EVENTS, CONFERENCES AND CONVENTIONS

Have you ever stopped to count all of the artisan food festivals and tastings that you participate in every year? The number is mind-boggling. Virtually every major market hosts some kind of festival like this, and you could spend your life simply going from one to the other.

Considering the participation costs of most these festivals and trade shows, it is critical to establish goals and develop cost-effective strategies for this kind of event. What kinds of goals are realistic? Well, let's start with the usual suspects. I have listed four goals often mentioned either singly or in combination by companies attending trade shows:

We want to find out what's going on in the industry, with customers, and with the competition. Taken alone, this is a poor reason to participate in a trade show. The same can be accomplished by simply attending the show, without the costs of exhibition space. And for that matter, if you don't know what's going on in the industry, by the time it is the talk of the trade show, it's way too late for you. You should be using market research, not industry gossip, in your decision-making process.

On the other hand, once your participation is indicated by one of the goals below, this becomes a legitimate secondary goal—one that takes advantage of the concentration of industry representatives and customers.

We want to "show the flag." This is a difficult goal to achieve because it is so hard to quantify. What is the benefit of "showing the flag"? Only very large companies wishing to maintain their corporate image as important players (leaders in the category) should use this as a reason for participation in a trade show. For the rest of us, showing the flag is simply another way of saying "we have no measurable goals for this event, but don't want to miss it if something important happens." That's not a goal I can endorse.

We want to make sure our competition doesn't get an advantage. This goal is often combined with the first two goals above in a very defensive approach to justify participation. In other words, "We can't leave the field open to our competition, so we must be there." Of course, this ignores the more obvious question, "Even if your competition isn't there, what do you expect to achieve?"

The sad truth about this approach is that it neglects more meaningful goals, and often leads to half-hearted efforts and poorly conceived plans. This is especially true when the axiomatic assumption is made that since we have low expectations, we should invest little money, thought, or time into planning or strategy for the event.

We really need to make more sales or media contacts. This is by far the best reason to participate in industry trade shows. It is measurable, contributes directly to the bigger picture, and can have lasting impact. But if this is the goal, how many companies actually develop a specific strategy to achieve it? Not many. But you should do exactly this. That means you have to answer the following questions:

How much will participation cost in terms of time, money, and materials? Please don't forget to include product costs, travel time, T&E budgets, and all associated costs.

Charity auctions offer real opportunities to create awareness of your brand and products

How big is the payoff? How many contacts (and of what importance) will we need to make to justify these expenses?

This doesn't mean that the sales contacts you make at the show have to place orders large enough to pay for the costs of the show within three months. That's not how marketing communication works. Some of those contacts won't pay those kinds of dividends for a while. But you do need to look at these events as investments—and you do need to understand how that investment is going to pay off. If you don't have a way to track these investments, how can you possibly make good decisions about them?

Clearly, the staff attending the trade show should agree on a measurable goal for a specific number of sales contacts to be made, as well as a target number of follow-up sales calls and orders placed. By tracking these numbers and the success of the attending staff, a much more refined sales plan can be developed that will make future decisions easier and more accurate.

A spreadsheet is the way to go. Under the heading of your costs, list sample product costs, staff time costs, travel costs, and any fees you might have to pay to participate. Add those up and look at the total.

Then make a list of all the contacts you hope to make: How many journalists will you talk to? Distributors? Restaurateurs? Retailers? And how many consumers will you convince to visit your farm/production facility, join your club, or sign up for your newsletter?

Now compare those two summaries: Is the event really worth it? If so, full speed ahead. But make sure that you provide the people working the event with a spreadsheet to track all the contacts you expect them to make. That allows them to keep track, and measure their success against your forecast.

By having a stated goal, your staff can focus on making sure those numbers are reached. Such an approach should also encourage the sales and marketing team to explore other, more cost-effective methods of achieving these same goals. The result will be a professional and results-oriented approach to the often time-intensive process of sales calls. Trade shows are only one means to the end, and a good PR professional will explore a wide range of tactics to achieve any goal.

Of course, as in all marketing communications, the secret here is to know your audience. Before you participate in a festival or trade show, answer these questions:

Who is the audience and what do they want?

This must be determined BEFORE the trade show. Your sales and marketing team should develop a profile of the contacts who plan on attending the show. These profiles should indicate special interests, products, or budgets that are of concern to those attending. This information should then be referenced against the marketing goals of the company to develop a plan for each trade show. Who is going to be there, and what do they want?

What can we do to get their attention?

Now that we know who they are and what they want, we can begin to develop a trade show booth and activities that will attract the target market and encourage them to spend time with us. We are not preparing for a party; we are designing a campaign—one with a budget, objectives, and the potential for both failure and success.

Use Advance Direct Mail to create interest in your booth, and to get a head start on making the key contacts. Most shows will offer to sell a list of those attending to any exhibitor. Such a list can often be used very effectively to encourage a visit to the company's booth,

**Banner for Union des Grands Crus de Bordeaux
trade tasting**

follow up on a marketing communication package presented at the show, or even pre-select attendees according to need or interest. If you know what you want to accomplish, then using this service to advertise your intentions, or to pre-screen visitors to your table can be really effective.

In a recent trade tasting we organized, some of the participants were disappointed that they didn't get to spend more time with the key trade visitors. Why? Because two of the industry leaders had done their home-work, and invited most of the top attendees to meet with them about future business plans. The others were left talking to the less influential visitors who were left.

Host a Hospitality Suite in the same hotel, or nearby, to give your key contacts a place to meet with you away from the distractions of the show. Often, the trade show floor itself is an overwhelming experience for potential customers. Offer these customers an interesting reason to leave the crowded floor and join you in a more relaxed and focused setting in a hospitality suite in the same hotel. This kind of participation can be done without the fees for exhibition booths, and will generate an environment that allows you the undivided attention of the sales contact. Offers of a more social place to meet with one's spouse, entertainment, or other incentives will draw the customers to your suite.

This isn't as easy as it sounds. Drawing customers away from the festival floor to your suite requires a great deal of contact work by the company's sales staff to meet the potential customers and constantly remind them of the opportunity that awaits them in the hospitality suite. That means hard work and preparation.

Organize interactive events at the trade show to generate more attention for your company.

These can be anything from "star attractions" to private dinners—anything that will give the sales contacts something to talk about and a reason to visit with you. The main drawback of most of these attempts is that they depend on borrowed interest; the contact is not interested in your company or products, but in the event. As a result, sales contacts are not always genuine, nor are they motivated.

On the other hand, the special dinners you organize should be planned well in advance, and executed against the stated goal. They are not just an excuse for your marketing team to spend its T&E budget by taking a bunch of colleagues to a nice restaurant—although that is what usually happens.

Which leads us to the development of a spectacular trade show booth as a way of effectively generating interest and enthusiasm in your company. Of course, many of the key events do not allow you to bring your own booth. But there are a few basic rules that can be applied to all trade show booths (some can be applied to any marketing communications materials) that must be understood:

The booth and its design must be symbolic of the quality and character of your company. If you are making a claim to preemptive

Trade tasting

leadership, you must have a trade show booth that supports your position—both in content and in style.

Thus if you want to be perceived as a major player, you must have a large, imposing booth. If you want to be seen as a cost-effective alternative, your booth must show the kind of clever, creative thinking that allows for cost-effective solutions without a loss of quality.

Finally, the staff and materials must be consistent with your corporate philosophy and your target audience. Do not use gorgeous teenage models to sell baby food, and don't use slickly attired high-pressure salespeople to sell a handcrafted artisan product.

The average time spent at a trade show booth is fifteen seconds. At the end of that time, the viewer moves on to another booth unless he is given a reason to stay. Certainly a discussion with your sales staff will accomplish that goal, but your sales staff can only speak to one person at a time. You must give other potential customers something to do while they wait.

At major festivals, I like to position the company owner or principal out in front of the booth, where he/she can track down key contacts and interact with important industry leaders. The PR or sales staff handles staffing the booth itself, so that the principal isn't trapped behind the table (and a crowd of consumers) when the most important journalist at the event walks on by—and doesn't stop to taste your products.

In the final analysis, the results you achieve will depend on the efforts of your sales staff, and you should do all you can to give them the kinds of materials and environment that allows them to concentrate on selling your products.

Your staff can make all the difference. Clearly, this will be a key element in your success. If there is one basic rule of trade show participation, it is that staff sitting down in chairs behind tables will never be successful. Your staff must be approachable, outgoing, and positioned in a way that places no barriers between them and the sales contacts. Your booth must be open, well-lighted, and must encourage contacts to enter your area and meet you, face to face.

Choose staff because they know the customers. Nothing can improve upon a salesman who has already established rapport with potential customers. This personal relationship can make contact easier, follow-up more effective, and closing more frequent.

Choose staff because they know the market. Knowledge and credibility should be chosen over a pretty face every time, because once you get a live sales prospect, the last thing you want to do is put him/her on hold while you go find someone who knows the business.

Choose your staff because of their ability to evaluate the trade show and make suggestions for future improvements in your booth, your participation, and your products.

Make sure your staff has agreed to the goals for the trade show, and hold them responsible for achieving them. Encourage them to suggest improvements in both the booth and their own efforts that will generate more success.

At that same trade show I mentioned above, one if the companies' reps complained that they hadn't made a single sale. "I just don't think there are any buyers here," he said. His neighbor at the next table waited until we had a moment alone before he confided that he had just sold a full container of product to someone at the show. "The buyers are here," he said, "but you have to know what they want. We brought special products for this show because we did some research in advance, and knew what they were looking for."

That advance preparation, born out of their focused strategy, gave immediate and positive results.

But wait, there's more. After the show you have to follow up quickly and effectively with every sales contact. Without the proper execution of this single element, the world's most exciting booth and sales staff will fail to produce any results at all. And to make this even easier, it's a good idea to incorporate some kind of a promotion into your participation in the trade show itself—a reason to follow up on every contact—and a reason for them to look forward to that follow-up. Whether it be free gifts or in-situ demonstrations, the reason for these follow-up visits is to keep the door open for future contacts and future sales. More on this later in the chapter.

Most important, use the time after the show to evaluate your efforts. What can you improve? Was the show worthwhile? Why? What will you do next year to achieve your goals? And how will you adjust your expectations for next year?

What about hosting an event at the company?

I was recently asked to look at a winery property as a potential investment opportunity. One of the first things out of the real estate agent's mouth was that the property had permits for just about any kinds and numbers of events you wanted to hold. The agent rightly suggested that this was a very solid source of potential revenue.

What he didn't mention was how much work and money such events entailed.

I have come to see special events on the company property as one of the least understood elements of any public relations campaign, right up there with media relations. The reasons for this are three-fold:

Most companies don't define the goals for their events.
Most companies don't create the specific events to accomplish specific goals.
Most companies don't evaluate events against other potential marketing communications options.

Or, in simpler terms, they don't know what they are doing, they don't know how to do it, and they don't know whether it's worth the money they're spending on it.

That sounds like a recipe for disaster, doesn't it?

As usual, I have a few suggestions that will help you avoid the most obvious of these mistakes, and then let you worry about what's really important, like whether the shrimp or crab entrée is better!

What's the goal?

All too often, the goal of a special event is to "create a really memorable experience." I always have to ask the obvious question: For whom? You cannot define the goal of a special event until you define the audience, and most companies don't define this very carefully. They want to throw a good party; they want to send everyone home happy, with an enhanced vision of what the company's style is.

The problem is that they invite a wide range of people, each of whom has his or her own sense of style. In the end, this just becomes another party that the owners enjoy and hope their friends do as well. And it generally costs a fortune.

To define the goal effectively, you have to define the audience. As in all public relations programs, the publics can really vary. A distributor event should be pretty darn different from a consumer event. And an event aimed at the media will, by definition, need to be different from one for the local community.

And no, you can't do all things for all people. Abe Lincoln already explained that.

For the media, you will want a fairly exclusive event—something that allows the media to experience something beyond what the normal consumer might find. Large walk-around tastings with hundreds of people and a rock band generally don't attract media. In fact, many journalists will ask about the event before agreeing to attend. If it sounds too crowded, you won't get many takers. For some in the media, an exclusive scoop is quite important. Inviting them to an event with six other writers will automatically convince them not to write—because six other writers will already have the story.

You can sometimes ameliorate this effect by having the writers meet with different people and have different experiences at the same event. A trade writer might sit with the marketing director to learn about new sales initiatives, while a society writer might want to write about who else is attending, and a food writer could go back into the kitchen to interview the chef. But in general, that's a complicated recipe. You are better off reaching out to writers individually and giving them the experience they can really use to write a story. And frankly, that rarely involves being invited to large parties.

On the other hand, if you invite a single writer to attend a private party with the owners, and that writer gets a story in a major magazine, the effort might well be worth the cost of the entire event. That's a good investment!

Distributors and other members of the trade are another kettle of fish entirely. Your goal here should not be to give them the fully illustrated history of your company, complete with a tasting of all of the products. They don't have the attention span for that, and they won't remember half of it anyway. What you want to do here is to create a personal relationship with a few of the salespeople. Instead of taking the group to a concert (or hosting a concert) with a big name artist, what you really want is a golf tournament or bocce ball championship that allows your team to spend a lot of one-on-one time with these key members of your sales team.

Forget the Big Show, and focus on quality time with this audience. What you are building here are long-term relationships based on hours of time together. Doing things together is always better than just watching things. For this group, family-style dining is better than table service, because it forces the people to interact with each other. That's the point.

If you ever thought of combining the trade with the media, please don't. When your salesman in Alabama starts complaining about the fact that he doesn't get enough support for the on-premise market, or your top retailer in Atlanta asks you to reduce prices because your products aren't moving there, you don't want a writer listening to the conversation. Ever.

Which brings us to the last major audience, consumers. I would suggest that there are three kinds of consumer events that you might consider, and each one has a very different focus and purpose.

Building Traffic

The most obvious kind of event is one that simply encourages foot traffic/car traffic to the company's sales/tasting room—to create a sense of destination for consumers. We've all seen a lot of these kinds of events, from participating in a "passport weekend" to jazz concerts, art exhibitions, and even bike races and marathons. As you might expect, I am skeptical of these events, unless I can see a careful evaluation system in place.

Is the goal to get a lot of people on the property? Why? I fully support such events if they are self-supporting, generate a positive image for the company, and encourage those attending to buy product and join your club. At the end of the day, if you can say that the event was self-supporting and enhanced the image of the company, then I suggest you move full speed ahead with more of the same.

When the events cost money, the goal you achieve must be worth that expenditure. Hosting a huge event to gain seven club memberships and to sell an extra nineteen cases of product is not a good equation, in my mind. When you cost out the event, be brutally honest in your evaluation of staff time, advertising costs, and the like. It is particularly easy to suggest that your tasting room staff doesn't have anything better to do than work on special events, but if that is the case, the problem is that your tasting room staff isn't properly managed. The solution isn't to create work for them planning special events. The solution is to manage their time and energy in a way that really sells your product.

But in most cases, these events cost a lot of money, staff time, and energy. What kinds of marketing campaigns could you organize if you began with those budgets of time? If you had a budget of thousands of dollars, and countless hours of staff time, could you sell more in your tasting room and sign up more club memberships? I think we all know the answer to that one.

Charity Events

Of course, there is a way to dodge this bullet a bit. If you choose to host a charity event, you can often pass most of the costs of the event on

Sponsoring a local charity event is a cost-effective way to raise your local profile while doing some good

to the charity organization, and still achieve some of the same goals. Yes, you do share the attention and positive image with the charity, but for most companies, that's a good thing.

The drawback to this arrangement is that most charities host events to make lots of money. The more costs you pass on to them, the less money they make. It's a delicate course to sail if you are going to really give them the support they want, and still limit your financial exposure for the event.

Happily, you have something to sell beyond just your product. By offering tours, private tastings, and other such amenities, you can help generate funds for the charity without blowing the marketing budget completely out of the water.

I would like to point out one issue here concerning charity fundraisers. I draw a very clear distinction between charity fundraising events and charity community building events. A bake sale builds community. Everyone participates, and everyone feels good about his or her participation. But a bake sale is no way to raise $300,000. If you want to raise that kind of money, you really need to design the event in a different way. And you don't get to feel good about participating—you get to feel good about raising lots of money. Don't make the mistake of thinking your event can do both, because it probably can't.

Community building events are very effective, but you should be clear about that goal. Most companies do not spend enough time and energy on their local community-building efforts. It is so easy to sit in your office, waiting for the donation requests to pile up on your desk. But that doesn't build community.

What builds community is getting involved. Working with people is so much more effective than simply giving them free product. I think all companies should have the goal of improving their relationships with their neighbors, their local officials, and their larger employee/local services family. It may be as simple as a "bring your own protein" barbecue, or a clean up the river day. And it should involve as many of your employees (and owners!) as you can possibly involve, working side by side with all of the potential members of these target audiences.

And it is much more cost-effective than donating all those individual product samples, and advertising in all those local programs.

Private Parties

If you are lucky, you might even have a use permit that allows a wide range of events on the premises, including using the property itself as a revenue source. You can host weddings, private parties, and receptions that not only expose the company and its products to a broad range of people, but also generate profits for the company.

This is a good thing, sometimes.

If you have a crack events coordinator who can attract the right kinds of people, this can not only generate profits; it can also create a truly enhanced image for the brand. A private dinner for Nobel Prize winners, an exclusive reception for season ticket holders at the opera, or a local reunion for the Harvard Business School graduates in your area would all do the trick nicely.

A workshop on cost cutting for the managers of Wendy's restaurants might not have the same beneficial effect on your image. Plan accordingly.

There is another risk involved in these kinds of events. Most artisan producers are going to live or die by the quality of their products and their marketing. If you take on special events as a key element to your identity, you must then do as professional a job on those events as you would on everything you make. If your core competency is cheese, you should be very careful when you expand that to include special events. If you can't do them perfectly, you run the risk of ruining your reputation.

If you choose to go this route, bear in mind that your competition is no longer a competitor down the road, but the Ritz-Carlton Hotel or the local country club. And some of them are pretty good at this kind of thing.

Whatever kinds of events you host, I strongly suggest that you make a habit of inviting your local official to attend them. Not only does this build the kinds of personal relationships that will help you in any number of ways, but it also is a very simple kind of insurance. When someone complains to the official about your party, at least that official can answer with a certain amount of accuracy about what happened there!

Take It On the Road

Of course, virtually all of these kinds of events can be adapted for use on the road. True, you will have to find a venue, but if the events really work, you can often do them in local hotels or restaurants around the country with similar results. In fact, that might be one of your criteria as you move forward with your event planning. Try to develop events that could become part of a national conference, or a distributor's outreach program for key accounts. It will force you to be more cost-effective, and it will force you to really focus on the goal. It may just force you to develop special events that really make sense, from every marketing and sales point of view.

In Summary

Events are so exciting that they often take on a life of their own. Budgets get amended, elements get added, and suddenly, instead of creating a little buzz about your new product release, you are launching a rocket to the moon. The only problem is that your company doesn't need a rocket to the moon—it needs to sell seven hundred cases of your new product.

Make sure your events don't become their own justification. Instead, build an event program exactly as you would build any marketing communications program: carefully, cost-effectively, and with an eye to how well the whole thing will work as you get larger. Design it to deliver specific goals and objectives, and be prepared to adapt it to meet the needs of a changing market or a revised budget.

And now a word about follow up:

How much time (and money!) do you spend working on your PR and marketing activities every year? If you are like most companies, that's a huge part of your job. You plan carefully. You develop a budget. You spend hours and hours on creative ways to promote your brand. You donate product, send out samples, mail press releases, and attend conferences and trade shows every month. You talk to the media, call on accounts, and interact with the public every chance you get.

Do you ever wonder why it isn't more effective?

It's because you are doing everything right except one. You are planting the seeds and watering the crops. You just aren't harvesting the fruit. You've created interest in the brand. You have made some kind of connection with every level of the distribution network, from distributor through the end consumer. You've smiled, shaken hands, and told stories. The only thing you haven't done is close the sale.

You haven't followed up.

Sure, I know why you haven't done it. You get back from a trip, and you are exhausted. And there is a pile of mail on your desk, and an endless stream of email on your computer. Your assistant needs guidance, your team needs direction, and you need a week off.

Those are not good excuses.

Communication is like dating. There is a rhythm to it, and it is important to hold up your side of the conversation. If you meet someone you like, you want to see them again. And that means you had better make sure that the communication stays alive. It's why you call, or send flowers, after a good first date. And when you meet someone in a business context, you should do the same.

No, you don't send them flowers. But you do follow up with them. You tell them how much you enjoyed meeting them, you remind them of an important topic of conversation, and you make it easy for them to tell you that they'd like to see you again.

It's good manners, but it's also brilliantly simple communications technique.

If you're like me, you get home from every big event with a pocket full of business cards, all of them given to you by someone you met—someone with whom you had a valuable conversation. What do you do with those? Put them in a file and feel good about the relationships you've built?

Wrong.

The day you get back in the office, you should pull out those cards and write every single one of those people a short note. It doesn't have to be a long and thoughtful missive. But if you met a restaurateur who said some nice things about your Chardonnay, you should write him to remind him of that—and ask him when you could come by for lunch, and deliver a couple of cases for him to offer by the glass. And if you met a food writer who was interested in your story about water conservation, you should follow up with a quick note that includes a link to some photos, and an invitation to visit the brewery and see what you are doing that is so special.

It's not being pushy; it's doing your job.

Most importantly, for every person you met and exchanged contact information with, you should send a note saying that you enjoyed meeting him or her, and that you look forward to future conversations. You should do this because it is true. You should also do this because it helps you build those very relationships that will pay dividends later. And you should do this because most other people won't—and this will serve to create a unique point of differentiation for you. You are the one who actually follows up.

This is not just true of big industry shows where you are meeting the members of the trade. You should also do this with your consumers! It is amazing to me that companies don't call their customers and talk to them. When a customer visits your tasting room and buys $138 worth of product, it's an important relationship for you. Within a week or two that customer should get a phone call from someone to say thank you. You can chat about the products, ask about their visit, and suggest a way to enjoy the food even more.

No, this is not junk mail, or telemarketing. It is building relationships with people who have already told you that they love you.

What store has the highest reputation for customer service in America? It's Nordstrom. And when you buy something nice at Nordstrom, you get a thank you card, and an invitation to call on your "private shopper" for exceptional and personal service.

Why wouldn't you do that at your company? It obviously works. Are you too busy to give personalized service? Then get out of the artisan food and beverage market. Or are you simply going to leave money, and good customer relationships, on the table?

Of course, the buzzwords in today's market are all about Social Media. Social Media is far more effective when it is based on an existing relationship. You need to take those relationships you have built through your marketing efforts over the year, and re-connect with them. And Social Media is perfect for this.

If you have a customer who loves your company, take their photo when they visit, and post it on your Facebook page. Even better, invite them to do it themselves. Write them an email. Thank them. Talk to them. Make them feel that you actually like them, rather than seeing them as merely a source of revenue.

Because for all that work you do throughout the year, you are not getting your money's worth, or your time's worth, if you are not following up. It turns out that the most important thing you can do to make all of your marketing successful is the last thing you do.

Follow up. Continue the relationship. And turn your contacts into friends, ambassadors, and missionaries for your brand.

CHAPTER 11

WHEN TO GET HELP FROM OUTSIDE—TRADE ASSOCIATIONS AND PR AGENCIES

Trade Associations: The Good, the Bad, and the Ugly

We all belong to them, from regional associations to the local Chamber of Commerce. And it seems that every week we are invited to join another one. On the face of it, these organizations offer a number of benefits: economies of scale, larger budgets, moral support, and safety in numbers. But those benefits are often outweighed by other factors.

Over my years in the business, I have seen many such organizations come and go, while others seemingly will live forever. What are the good ones? It may run counter to your first reaction, but sometimes the good organizations are not necessarily the best ones to join. And these decisions can often play a huge role in determining how successful your public relations efforts are going to be.

On the other hand, I am not interested in evaluating or rating every trade association available to those in the wine industry. I don't want to create the "great classification" of the year, nor do I want to listen to the complaints from those who feel that their organization was not rated fairly. I'll leave that to others in media whose skin is thicker—and who have more courage than I. But I hope you feel the decisions are easier to make after this article.

In the simplest of terms, what most producers want from a trade association is strength in numbers. They feel that if enough of their competitors band together to promote a product, or region, that this increase in time, energy, creativity, and money will help them achieve goals that they could not achieve as a single company. And the implication, at least, is that the benefits they reap from this association will outweigh their own contributions of time, energy, creativity and money.

Sadly, I don't think that is true very often.

Let's take a look at how these organizations usually work, and how you can get the most benefit from them.

The obvious advantage of any trade association is that it brings an already interested and focused audience to you. When you are trying to carefully target every marketing communications dollar, it's nice to know that the money you spend on ZAP is really going to reach people who are interested in Zinfandel. While USA Today or CNN reach a vastly larger audience, most of the people in that audience are not interested in wine, let alone old vine Zinfandel. That's a solid target audience for a specialized product.

The same can be said of an organization like Slow Food, for the same reasons. And if that organization is really energetic and dynamic, it can not only connect you with an existing audience interested in your specialized product; it can even play a role in increasing the overall market for that product.

Ultimately, then, a trade association can deliver two solid goals. It can put your message and product into the minds of a very targeted audience, and it may even be able to increase demand for a beverage category in your portfolio. Those are strong benefits.

But let's not forget the flip side.

When your trade organization reaches out and grabs that nicely targeted audience, it will deliver that audience to every one of your competitors in the category, as well. There is no better example of this than the annual ZAP tasting in San Francisco. As a Zinfandel producer, wouldn't it be great to be able to pour your wines for a horde of wine drinkers who love Zinfandel? Of course it would. But it would be even better if you didn't have to share the attention of those wine lovers with five hundred other producers of Zinfandel, all of whom are reaching out for the same kind of attention and recognition from that audience.

That's the pro and con in a nutshell: You get a beautifully targeted audience, but you have to share it with just about the entire category. Slow Food events attract just about every producer of artisan food in the area. That's a lot of competition.

And if the trade association does increase demand for the category, it is just as likely that it is also encouraging other companies and brands to enter into the category to compete with you. Does that make your life easier, or harder?

As always, the answer to the situation is based on your positioning and your ability to do a better job of taking advantage of the opportunities. Better than whom? Better than your competitors in that very association.

Does that sound just a bit too mercenary? Good. Marketing communications is mercenary, and your job is not to take delight in being out on the field with the other players; it is to get the ball and score. You are not on the field to play around; you are on the field to win the game.

At this point, I think we should start talking about a winning strategy for trade associations.

First, you need to develop specific goals for your participation in the organization. These should include goals for your company, as well as goals for the association as a whole. The goals should be both specific and measurable.

For your own company, your goals might include being included in fifty percent of all the stories written on the association or the category. If you are a major player, perhaps the goal should be one hundred percent of the stories.

Now that you have defined the goal, the next step is pretty obvious. You need to develop a strategy to achieve that goal. You must first make sure that you are notified about all such stories before they are written. That may fall under the auspices of the trade association, but if not, then you need to find another source for this information. And you

Examples of three trade associations

also need a very specific strategy to encourage the journalists writing that story to include you—often while excluding some of your category competitors.

How do you achieve that? You make sure that your story is better, that your information is more accurate, that your response is more timely, that your quotes are more memorable, and that your key individuals are more accessible to the media. It doesn't hurt if your products taste better, either.

Remember that journalists usually want news and they want trends. If you can show that you are breaking new ground, or capturing the essence of a change in the way Americans are drinking, then you have a better chance of getting included in the story.

Journalists also want people. People are behind every story in every publication, and when it comes to artisan food categories, we can almost predict who will get quoted. There will be a quote from the largest producer in the category. There will also be a quote from the most interesting personality in the category. It pays to spend a little time thinking of ways to say what you want to say in a clever and memorable way— although most completely ignore this advice.

And there will always be a quote from the current president of the trade association. It is certainly in your best interests to spend the time and energy necessary to become the president for a year. Once in office, you should make every effort to use the visibility that the office provides to reach out to the media and promote the category with all your heart— especially if your last name also just happens to be on your label.

What other kinds of goals might you define? For an association, you might aim to have retail shops create a special area dedicated to your region or product category—and then take very specific steps to achieve this goal in key markets across the U.S. Or you might simply aim to have every major food magazine in the U.S. publish a story about the category, complete with tasting notes on the leading producers.

In every case, the goal should be something that you can quantify—a final result that will translate into a real advantage in the marketplace. And as you do this, please don't forget to measure your success along the way. If you can identify a reason that your program is NOT working, that can be as valuable as achieving the goal. This is particularly true if you can do so early in the campaign. By identifying and eliminating a problem, you can then move ahead with a program that does work, and achieve the goals you have defined from the start. Without any such initial check, you can spend a lot of money on a campaign that is doomed to failure.

Of course, the other half of this equation has to do with money. Because it may be all well and good to achieve the kinds of goals we have identified in this article—but only if the cost of achieving those goals is within reason. Trade associations are not the only avenue to success, and everyone needs to evaluate the opportunity they present in relationship to all of the other possible strategies for achieving the same goals.

Don't overlook the economies of scale that trade associations can represent. By combining mailing lists and outreach programs, trade associations can help you distribute your message and build relationships with very interested members of the trade and consumers. A trade association website can help introduce your company and products to a larger audience that is already predisposed to buy within the category—and that should generate measurable results to your communications and sales goals. Even better, if your message is more memorable or effective than most of the other members', then you will benefit more than they will. Your time and money will be well spent.

When should you participate in a trade association? When the goals of the association are completely consistent with your own marketing and communications goals. When the association can offer a solid audience of interested consumers or trade. When the association may lack leadership or vision, opening the door for your own company to play a key and more visible role within the category. When the association offers the most cost-effective way to achieve the goals you have identified within your company. And finally, when your own company is simply not large enough to make any legitimate noise on its own.

But if that is the case, then you really can't expect the trade association to solve your problem. In that case, the trade association will offer you a wonderful opportunity to commiserate with a lot of other small companies that aren't category leaders and don't know what to do about it.

And speaking of getting help...

When should you hire a PR professional or a PR agency to help with the work? As with all really interesting questions, there is no single answer to this one, but there are ways to arrive at a conclusion. In the interests of helping you along that path, let's take a look at the lay of the land.

On our agency website, we have a nice clean statement about what we can offer our clients. It's not really different from what other agencies offer, but it serves perfectly as an outline for this discussion:

"When all is said and done, an agency can offer a client only three things:

- the expertise to do things well
- the time to do things right
- the creativity to make things fly"

If we take these items one by one, we should get a much clearer idea of how this works. And when we are done, we'll talk about how this compares to your in-house staff—current or future.

Expertise:

What kinds of expertise can a PR professional bring to the party? I've divided this into three rough categories: know how, know who, and know what.

Know How:

>> A PR professional knows the basics of PR and journalism—and it's taking care of those basics that makes the connection, in many cases, with the journalist on the other side of the fence. We know how to write a press release and media kit copy in classic A/P style, so that writers can use the material without extensive editing. That makes their lives easier, and gets you more coverage.

>> A PR professional knows the ins and outs of putting on major events, so that you don't have to sweat the details. That includes everything from understanding the negotiation process with the venue, to making sure that you have exactly the right kind of permit, to getting the product to the hotel the day before the event. These are the kinds of details that can make or break an event.

>> A good artisan industry PR professional knows the way publications work, so that you are included in the tasting they use to determine coverage. They know about the editorial

calendars and media submission policies for all kinds of different publications in the field.

>> A PR professional knows how to write a good story—and to adapt your information into the plot of a good story. That's often the difference between a feature length article about the company, and a mention of a single product that tastes good.

>> A PR professional also knows how to respond to a crisis, and develop a solid crisis management plan. I know this is not something you need today. It's something you may never need. But when you need one, you can't invent it on the spot. You are taking a risk by not having one.

In all of these areas, it really helps to have a PR professional on your side. He or she can improve your materials, increase your media coverage, and build better relationships with those pesky writers and bloggers. And that's what PR is all about, right? Which brings us to:

Know Who:

Media contacts are what everyone wants from a PR agency. And it's true that over the years I've been in business, I've managed to meet and even develop some pretty good relationships with media, both writer and others, across the country and even internationally.

But that is a lot different than saying that I can get a story placed anywhere I want, any time I want. In fact, most of my relationships are built on the idea that I NEVER try to force a story down a writer's throat. There is no point in that, unless you want to ruin the relationship for life. Instead, we strive to develop the kinds of relationships that allow us to work cooperatively with journalists to get them the stories THEY want. And then we work to include our clients. It's a longer-term approach to the business.

But no matter what kind of relationship we have with a writer, I can guarantee you one thing: A good story will trump a good relationship every time. No writer can afford to write second rate stories, and if you've got a story that really captures the imagination, you don't need a great PR agency to pitch it. A great story pitches itself—although a PR professional can help you improve your story, as per above.

Professionals in the PR business also know whom to call when they need information, testimonials, or key influencers in the market or with the media. Knowing which writers to call can really have an impact on the success of just about any story. That's a key element to any PR effort. Knowing the kind of tech support you need to do social media these days is an important part of the equation as well.

But there is one more element to the kind of expertise a PR pro can bring. Do you know what it is?

Know What

Because PR people are in constant contact with so many journalists and key influencers in the market, they have a pretty good idea of what is going on in the industry. They know what kinds of programs are working, and which are failing. They know some of the trends, and the hot buttons that get things started.

That's important, because all too often a small company has limited access to that information. A company can suffer from a limited vision of their marketing efforts. They need a sounding board that will give them an honest evaluation of what they are doing, and how it is being perceived.

Before you launch a new campaign, you need to know what stories would be of interest to the media, and which would not. And nobody knows this better than someone who has tried to pitch a hundred stories before.

Finally, there are a whole series of quirky elements to doing PR in this business. Every competition has a different set of regulations and requirements. Every state has different laws and fees. And most publications and writers have their own policies and prejudices. Knowing how these work can save you time, effort, and money.

Time

Remember when you were a kid, and people told you that time was money? You laughed. It's not funny anymore, is it? Time is the most valuable commodity we have, and most small businesses fight a constant battle to get things done. There are not enough hours in the day or years in a lifetime to finish the job.

This is where a PR pro can step in and make your life easier, and possibly better. First of all, all that expertise I've mentioned above really pays off when it's time to get the show on the road. While you and your team might spend hours (or years, for some projects) learning how to do something, a PR pro can step in and hit the ground running. By the time you might have figured the first step out, he or she will have wrapped up the whole package.

We also find ourselves doing a lot of things simply because our clients don't have the time to get things done. Over the years we have stepped in to take care of all sorts of administrative tasks that were falling by the wayside, and keeping the company from further success. This can be anything from entering competitions to answering consumer complaints, posting a blog, or writing back label copy. It's all part of keeping the ball moving, and because we've done it all before, we, like most PR pros, are pretty efficient about it.

Since we know how to do it, and have the time to do it, there is no need to reinvent the wheel. Which brings us to creativity.

Creativity

One of the toughest things about running a business is finding the time (yep, see above) to sit down and think creatively about your marketing communications plans for the future. All too often, the ideas that come up are the same ones you thought about two years ago.

That's where having someone from the outside step in and bring a fresh perspective is really valuable, and most PR pros love this part of the job. The secret to getting the best out of this input is to be VERY specific about the goals, and very UNSPECIFIC about anything else. Let them bring a wide range of ideas, activities and budgets to your table, and then see how they will fit with the rest of your plans. Too many restrictions up front just make creativity curl up and die. Give your professionals the room the exercise their creativity completely, please!

Best Practices

What would be best for you? Let's look at three scenarios that might work:

Should you hire an in-house PR pro, and turn over all over your PR problems to that one person? Maybe. A solid candidate for that job would be able to do a lot of what I have outlined here, and as their employer, you would have a hundred percent of their time and attention. The drawbacks might be that a single person probably doesn't have ALL this in one package. And they almost certainly won't be able to get it all done in a forty-hour work week. Then again, you might not need ALL of this right now.

Another option is to hire a PR agency and get all of this in one place. A good agency would bring the ability to execute on all of these fronts, from copywriting to social media. But it is unlikely that an agency would be able to provide all these services for the cost of a single employee. In other words, the agency can bring the whole package, but it will cost you!

There is a third option. You can tackle as much of this work as you can with your in-house staff, and then rely on an outside agency to fill in the blanks. Your employee could take on those projects best suited for his or her talent, expertise, and time. And the agency could fill in where you employee might have a weak spot, or a full calendar. And yes, it would be the best of both worlds. And it would cost more than just the employee alone.

As I said, there are no easy answers to complex questions. But if you use this chapter to define your priorities, you'll be taking a step in the right direction. Because there is one final option: You could do nothing. And that's not really an option at all.

CHAPTER 12

HOSTING CUSTOMERS, CLIENTS AND VIPS AT YOUR COMPANY

How many industries have thousands of consumers wanting to visit the factory every day? If you were to ask General Motors, Coca-Cola, or General Foods how they would feel about hosting hundreds of visitors a day, they would be delighted—especially if those visitors were willing to pay for the privilege, and would buy enough product to make the whole thing a profit center for the company!

Hospitality is a huge asset in our business, and there are relatively few companies that take full advantage of the opportunities that it offers. As you might imagine, I have a few suggestions on how to maximize every interaction with every visitor.

What Do Visitors Want?

First all, we have to get around that most basic question, because there are many kinds of visitors. To keep things simple, let's start out with two basic categories: the trade visitor, and the consumer. These are indeed two very different markets, and you should have a very different approach to each of them. First we will talk about how to deal with those most delicate of these audiences, the trade: distributors, retailers, restaurateurs, and their employees.

For the trade

If you are hosting a trade visitor, the key is defining expectations and then meeting them. The best place to start is with your own sales team. If they know what you have to offer, and can effectively explain that to any trade guests BEFORE they arrive, that's a huge step in the right direction. And that brings us to the first key to success for trade visitors:

Get as much information as you can about them before they arrive.

When we get a request for a trade visit, there is a series of questions that we want answered so that we can do our job well.

Who is the visitor, and what is their relationship to our company? Are they a buyer or merely a server at the restaurant? Do they currently carry the product, or are they just visiting a bunch of producers? Which products do they carry? Which ones should they carry? Are they traveling alone, or with their husband, girlfriend, extended family, or Boy Scout troop? We want to know how much wine they sell, and how big a part of their business is our company. Who is their distributor? Who is their sales rep? Have they ever visited us before? In short, we really want to know everything that the salesperson knows, so that we can do a perfect job of presenting ourselves in the best possible light.

That's a lot of information, which is why we use a standard visit request form that asks all of those questions. It is the sales team's job to fill in that form so that we can be prepared for the visit. In addition to all the info above, we also like to know where the visitor is staying, who they are visiting before us, and an emergency contact telephone number just in case something goes haywire.

From that form, we will work with the salesperson to define the kind of visit that is appropriate for the visitor. For a restaurant server and his family, we may choose to have them join a regular tour, and then join us in a separate room for a private tasting or two. For the owner of a distributorship, we will pull out all the stops, including a tasting of some special samples and a meal with the owner. But we can't make that decision if we don't get the information from the salesperson.

By the way, these forms are all on email, and as a result they are sometimes seen by the visitor, one way or another. That's a very good reason to use a code to distinguish between the various levels of hospitality. You don't want your visitor to say, "Oh, I see here that I am a level

The tasting room at Napa's Castello di Amorosa

two visitor. What does that mean? Who is a level one visitor, and what do they get?" Terms like "aficionado" and "gourmet" allow you to finesse that question without much difficultly.

Once the reservation is in place, we always like to confirm that reservation with a direct phone call from our hospitality staff to the visitor. It's a simple call, but it establishes a personal contact with the visitor. All that's needed is a short conversation, to explain that you are the host who has been assigned the coordination of the visit, and just want to confirm the basic information: who is coming, how many, and what time they will arrive. Just pretend you are a good restaurant confirming a reservation beforehand. By doing this, you also let the visitor know that you are paying attention and that your time is valuable. They might even call you if they are running late!

Once the visitor arrives, they should be greeted immediately by someone who knows that they are coming. They should be told that you've been expecting the visit, and that their host will be with them shortly. If the visitor arrives on time, that wait should certainly be less than five minutes.

What kind of tour should they get? Of course that all depends on the visitor. A couple of quick questions before you begin can be the difference between a great tour and a lousy one. It's a good idea to ask if the visitor has visited the area before, and if they have seen any competitors' companies. That way you can begin to achieve success in the area of key point #2:

If you find that they have visited many wineries in the past, you know that you can skip the stainless steel tanks and the bottling lines. Those are interesting once, but not more than that. If you learn that they have been touring in your area for three days, then you know that you can skip the part about the weather and the general soil types. Tailoring your presentation to their level of expertise and experience will make your tour a great deal more effective and enjoyable for everyone.

Sadly, most companies have a standard tour that they give, and it doesn't matter who the visitor is—that's the tour they are going to get. They will go on the same steady march that they did three years ago, the simple adoration of bottling lines that they were shown at the previous visits. They will be slightly bored. You will be, or should be, slightly alarmed. Yes, good people skills and the ability to tell a good story will keep the tour lively, but you are missing a huge opportunity here.

I was once asked to give a tour to a group of trade visitors, and I noticed that the leader of the group was a legendary expert. The last thing I wanted to do was insult him with a basic tour, but I was at a loss as to how to handle the situation. Luckily, as I started to explain the tour, it occurred to me to ask the expert his opinion of the process. He quickly jumped in with a long explanation of the factors involved. The guests were charmed. I was off the hook. And the expert was delighted. At each new stage of the tour, I quickly turned to the expert for his advice and opinion, and the tour was a huge success. In fact, he later wrote a letter saying it was the best tour that he had ever been given!

If you have good background information about your visitors, and you combine that with a quick series of questions to establish what they want to see and do, you are well on your way to a good hospitality experience. But so many companies fail in the next step. Despite the interest that some consumers might show in the basic tour, that's not good enough for any trade visitor. You have to edit your material and deliver only the key points. Remember that most people forget ninety percent of what they hear. So don't tell the trade how you make your product; just tell them what makes you special. Which brings me to key point number two for the trade visitor:

Only show your visitors what is different or new about you and your company.

This is where your key message for the brand has to stand out. Trade visitors have seen just about everything, and usually more than once. While they are polite, what they are really interested in learning is simple: What can you do for me, and what makes your products so special? Trust me, temperature-controlled stainless steel tanks or a room full of cheese is not the answer to either of those two questions!

The visit should be orchestrated so that every stop in the tour helps illustrate the power and truth of your key marketing message. (If you don't know what that is, go back to the first chapter, and start reading from there!)

I was recently in Bordeaux, where I joined a group of wine experts in a visit to Château La Tour Blanche in Sauternes. The visit was a perfect example of how to manage a group of wine experts. The tour group was composed of judges at the Concours Mondial de Bruxelles—some of the top wine judges in the world. When we arrived at Château La Tour Blanche, we were greeted by the director of the winery, who gave us a very quick history of the winery itself. (Donated to the government by the owner in the early 1900s, the winery is now run as both a winery and school for training students in enology.) This was followed by a very informal summary of how Sauternes is made—informal because we were all wine experts, and had heard these stories before.

And then, instead of marching us through the vineyards, or making us shiver as we admired tanks, we were presented with a long table covered with wine bottles. On the table were two bottles each of every one of the twenty-six classified growths of Sauternes from the 2007 vintage, in alphabetical order. As the director of La Tour Blanche explained, "We thought that you might enjoy the opportunity to taste through the classified growths of Sauternes all at one time, so that you could really understand the stylistic difference and range of these wines. Tasting glasses are on the table behind you. Please enjoy yourselves."

We did. And she earned huge bonus points for understanding who we were, and what our interests really were. Pencils were flying, notebooks were crammed with notes…and when we got back on the bus, we were all thoroughly impressed.

Which brings me to the fourth key point:

Give them an experience to remember

Talking at people is a lot more fun for the talker than the talkee. And no tour guide, no matter how good, can compete with an experience to remember. If at all possible, get the visitor to do something interactive. Have them make a blend, taste some of the raw material, or play a game of hoops with the owner. All of that is more fun than a technical discussion of production methods.

We once organized an event for a group of high-end food and wine bon vivants and trade visitors. In competition with a number of wineries that organized black-tie dinners, we invited our guests to join us in the vineyard, where we showed them how to plant a grapevine. They teamed up with one of our vineyard workers, and learned all the steps required to successfully plant a grapevine.

They loved it. Most of the groups planted two or three vines, and then we led them off to a lovely barbecue lunch in the trees near the vineyard. But one group of visitors, dressed in their Sunday best, lagged far behind. I finally went back to encourage them to join us for lunch. "No thanks," they said. "We want to finish the row!"

That's an experience they will remember long past the discussions of rootstocks and drainage. In fact, the winery continued to hear from some of those visitors for years, as they checked up on their grapevines to see how they were growing.

And that leads us to key point number five.

Follow up on the visit with good information.

The visit isn't over when the visitor leaves. After the visit, the host should put together a report on the visit. That report should include what products they tasted, the questions asked, and opinions voiced by the visitor. In the best of all possible worlds, the report should include a couple of products that the visitor wants to buy right now. And that report should go out within twenty-four hours of the visit. It should go to the local distributor sales rep, as well as the company sales team. It is the final link in the chain that builds better sales, better relationships, and better results for everyone.

If you take care of all five of these key points, your trade hospitality program will generate great results, and will give you a competitive edge in the marketplace. Because hospitality isn't just about being nice—it's about winning the war for a share of the customer's mind.

It's pretty clear that for most artisan producers, the future of food and beverage sales and marketing is right in their own front yard. With the proliferation of new companies, products, and brands, and the limited number of distribution companies in any given market, it's very hard for a small producer to gain effective national or even regional distribution.

On the other hand, there are any number of companies in the U.S. that are making a living by selling plenty of product through their tasting room, loyalty club, and retail operations. And these sales are at full SRP (Suggested Retail Price), and not discounted by fifty percent to sell through a wholesaler.

Obviously, your tasting room is an extremely important part of your sales network. It may be your ONLY sales network. But a tasting room is a lot more than just an opportunity for sales. It's also an opportunity to interact with many of the publics that should be addressed in your public relations programs. And it is amazing to me how many opportunities are missed by companies who could and should know better.

Your Most Important Public: Your Employees

Never overlook the importance of your employees as one of your key publics. They are the interface with your customers, and how they manage that communication has a huge impact on your business. But I'll bet you don't take full advantage of this key audience.

At least once a month, your employees should get a one-hour staff training that helps them understand more about the company, its products, and its communications goals. Yes, this should include a tasting of any new product releases. But it should also include updates on key marketing initiatives, as well as education and training on any issues you are facing from a local community point of view.

If you let your employees know more about the new products, they will sell more of them. If you keep them up to speed on your marketing efforts, they will be able to support them more effectively. And if you train them on the issues you are facing in your local community, they can help you both build your image and combat negative impressions. But you have to give them all the information they need, and the support to do this well. That means education and training.

Neighbors

No one can make your life more difficult than your next-door neighbor. And yet many companies often do not do a good job of building a positive and long-lasting relationship with the people who live next door. That's a huge mistake.

The first step? Stop and listen. Neighbors will be happy to tell you what their fears and complaints are, but you have to be willing to listen to them. And trust me, if you don't, they will find a local official who does. Then your problems will multiply many times over.

I recommend inviting your neighbors to attend any events that you host, free of charge. And giving them a discount at the tasting room. And hosting a community reception/meeting once every six months or so to give them a chance to chat with you—and you a chance to listen to them.

None of that is as important as stopping by when you see them in their front yard, asking them how things are going, and then listening.

Local Officials

If you don't contact local officials, both elected and regulatory, they will certainly contact you. But if you do it first, you will often be able to establish a much better foundation for any future relationship. Don't wait for them to come calling because of a complaint or concern; take the initiative and invite them to visit, show them what you are doing, and give them a tour of your operations.

It's simply good preventative medicine.

Local Competition

Speaking of people who can make your life harder, your local competitors are in a very good position to do that. They know the laws better than your average neighbor, and your success may even breed envy in their ranks.

The solution is to take the initiative and host them, as a group, and make them feel as if they are part of your audience—because they are. Hosting an informational discussion group once a month about issues of common interest is a great way to build rapport, and it can create some additional opportunities. Don't forget that the Napa Valley Vintners Association, the most powerful organization of its kind in America, began just this way—as a group of about five to seven winery owners who met for lunch on Tuesdays.

And as the host of such meetings, you are also positioning yourself as a local industry leader. That's good.

Local Accounts

One of the best sources of new customers for any company is the list of local restaurants and retail shops. Even if you don't sell to those businesses, you should host an event at least once a year when they are all invited to come visit you. Tell them your story, show them a good time, and make sure they taste all of your products. It will only help drive referral business over the long haul.

Media

You almost never have news, so it's often hard to get the attention of the media, whether they be local or international. But that doesn't mean that you shouldn't talk to them. At least once a quarter you should have a conversation with your local newspapers, just to make sure that they know who you are. Tell them about the kinds of things you are doing locally (you might even invite them to some of the meetings and events described above), and you might even get some coverage. At the very least, you will establish a relationship that will help you communicate with them more effectively when they do call—about that complaint from your neighbor!

Your Customers

Yes, I've saved the best for last. There is no better source of new business than your existing customers. They already know who you are, and they like you. But do you know why? Your tasting room is the perfect place for some nice market research that will help you understand what you are doing right, and what you need to improve. And DO NOT assume that you know these answers! I have never done a market research project that didn't generate at least some surprises for my clients.

You can do this research more formally, by inviting your customers to fill out a questionnaire. (You can reward them with a discount or the chance to win an invitation to a private event.) If the questionnaire is good, and you get enough people to fill it out, you can learn an astonishing amount about your customers and what they think about you—the kind of knowledge that marketing giant Procter & Gamble would spend a fortune to know.

Or you can do it informally, by training your tasting room staff to ask the right questions. The results here are much harder to tabulate, but that just means that you should limit the number of questions, and keep them simple. Instead of one large questionnaire, ask your staff to just spend one week asking every customer a single question. Over time, if you do this right, you will get the information you need to be much more successful. And you will make your customers feel as if they are not just customers, but part of your team.

That is good PR.

And now a note about women: It's all about sex

Recently I was invited to make a marketing presentation to a conference aimed at exploring the best way to sell artisan products in a broad range of circumstances, from distributor presentations to the tasting room.

What they didn't know is that I was up to my usual tricks. Once we had completed my presentations, I asked the audience to break up into small groups of four or five people, and each group was instructed to develop a marketing and sales pitch for a product they had never seen before. They were given about ten minutes for the whole process.

Who says marketing is slow?

It was the perfect opportunity for them to put into practice all of the concepts and theories that I had presented over the course of the day, and they dived into the exercise with great enthusiasm.

But when it came time to hear their pitches, it was my turn to be surprised!

The first speaker was a woman who got carried away with a wild and romantic pitch about her product. That was followed by a more rational man who gave a very accurate set of tasting notes on the product itself. Then another woman spoke, and she talked about the seductiveness of the flavors involved, and provided a series of fascinating food pairings. A man presented the next one, once again with an accurate set of tasting and production notes.

Are you beginning to see a pattern here?

Yep. Every time a woman presented, she talked about romance and style, food and fun. She clearly had adopted the product as a part of her lifestyle. And every time a man presented, he talked about how it was made, and specific notes about color, flavor, balance and finish.

In short, the men were describing the product. The women were describing how the product made them feel.

In advertising, the men were talking about features. "The product is this, and the product does that." The women were talking about benefits. "I like it because it does this for ME! I like it because I feel good when I use it!" And there is a very old and very good advertising maxim: Talk about benefits, not features.

Deborah Tannen, Ph.D., in her book *You Just Don't Understand,* does a wonderful job of explaining how men and women use communication differently to accomplish what are obviously different objectives. I will try to paraphrase some of her findings here, but would strongly suggest that you read the book—it is thoughtful, convincing, and thoroughly entertaining.

Tannen says that women use communication and language to build rapport and create community—to draw people together and build a sense of trust and sharing. Men, on the other hand, generally use communication to establish a chain of command, to report information and to reinforce a social hierarchy.

Those are pretty different objectives, and in practice they lead to some pretty clear difficulties. In one particularly effective passage, Tannen uses the example of a man who returns to his home after a hard day at work. His wife, as a way of establishing rapport and building community, reaches out to him and asks him how his day went. The man responds grimly and tersely. After all, she is not his supervisor, and he doesn't report to her!

While that may be an extreme example, I have often seen a woman ask a question, only to be provided with information she doesn't want and can't use. The man is using the situation to establish his role as the expert, the superior in this relationship. He is now in control. He is mansplaining. Instead of getting an invitation, she gets an education. She is wiser, but she isn't happier—and she doesn't buy the product!

(In another memorable experiment, Tannen asks two small girls to carry chairs into a room and then sit down and talk. The girls place the chairs so close together that they are almost touching knees, and then lean forward to talk to each other. Boys in the same study carefully place the chairs side by side, facing the same direction, so that they can look at the wall while they talk. It's amazing that the two sexes manage to get along at all!)

As I look over the history of the artisan food and beverage market in America, I see a constant theme in most marketing communications campaigns: They almost all spend a lot of time talking about features, and very little time talking about benefits. It's as if they never read a book about advertising or marketing.

Some of this may be based on the classic misconception of the market in general, that men are the target market. That's just not true.

If you study the Constellation Wines Genome Project—the study of the psychographics of the American wine consumer—you quickly see that in five of the six primary market categories, the majority of wine consumers are women. For other artisan food products, that ratio is going to be even higher.

That shouldn't be earthshaking news. Anyone who has studied the market over the past twenty years knows that women do most of the shopping in the U.S. And no, this isn't just in supermarkets. And that doesn't look like it is going to change any time soon.

In fact, the Constellation Genome study actually suggests that men collect individual bottles of wine, while women buy wine to drink on a regular basis. Which is the more attractive consumer? I think that is pretty obvious.

(Yes, there are statistics that show that in the Millennial Generation the split is more even, and may even favor men by a small percentage. While that trend may speak to a generational change that will continue as the Millennials age, I don't think so. I think that as they get older, and these young men and women get married, and start having children, many of the old gender roles will surface. Women will tend to stay at home with the children more than men do, and as a result will also do more of the shopping. My two Millennial daughters will give me a first row seat to see if this is true.

No, I am not a reactionary sexist. I am not making value judgments about this. I am just trying to predict the future, based on my experiences with the past. If you have a better extrapolation system, then let's hear it!)

Even if these figures do change, it will take at least a generation, or thirty years, for them to come true. So why are we still talking to the men, instead of the women?

More importantly, why are we talking to men in a way that actually excludes and repels women, rather than trying to speak a language that would, at the very least, be acceptable, effective, and attractive to both genders?

Good question.

I am not writing this as a radical feminist. I will not burn my bra. But isn't this the craziest system you ever saw? When you look at other industries that sell primarily to women, you find that there is a very strong contingent of women in every position of authority. Cosmetics? Fashion? Magazines? All those industries have women in highly visible and responsible roles across the board. And yet in our industry, the exception is the rule, and we can all identify a few women who play important roles. We can identify them because they stand out—they are memorable because they are such a rare commodity.

In the National Football League, it took a regulatory change from the league office for teams to start hiring African American head coaches. One wonders what it will take to accomplish the same kind of progress in the wine industry.

So what should we do?

Certainly, we should interview and hire qualified women in marketing and sales roles. But one of the sad relics of our past is that our distribution system is still mainly populated by men. The situation holds us all back, and prevents us from having more and greater success.

You should also read Leslie Sbrocco's excellent book *Wine for Women*. The title may be a bit misleading, because this is really much more than a guide for women interested in exploring the world of wine. It's a guide to how women think about food, wine, and other artisan products. It's an entertaining read, and it will really open your eyes.

In it, Sbrocco explains that women buy these products as a way to express their sense of personal style, and to capture their mood on a given day or for a given event. For women, a purchasing decision isn't so much about how the product is made, but about how the brand makes them feel. Women understand why they need the perfect little black dress, those kicky stiletto high heels, and the everyday handbag. And they use many of those same criteria to select the perfect dish for a girls' night out, or a formal dinner with the boss. As Sbrocco writes about it, it makes perfect sense.

So how many of us use those terms to sell their wine?

Exactly.

I once asked Leslie to make a presentation to a large dinner in Chicago. One of my clients, the Union des Grands Crus de Bordeaux, was the featured partner at a massive and formal dinner at the Field Museum of Natural History. It was a gala affair, and everyone who loved fine Bordeaux was there.

The château owners had carefully selected three beautiful wines to pour with the dinner, and had asked three well-known wine experts to present the wines at dinner. But then one of the three experts was ill, and sent his regrets. They needed a pinch hitter.

I suggested Leslie.

And after some suitable resistance, she finally agreed.

What happened next was truly remarkable. The first two speakers, both exceptional experts with enormous knowledge, gave wonderfully in-depth presentations about their respective châteaux. They talked about soils and geology, slopes and exposure, and every element of the winemaking procedure. If you were going to take an academic exam on the châteaux, this was the perfect information download for your test.

Leslie was a pinch-hitter, and did not have the same time to prepare. Rather than try to bluff her way through the presentation, she was both honest and charming. She admitted that she couldn't give the same kind of detailed information about the wine that the previous two speakers had provided, and she apologized for that.

And then she led us on a tasting of the wine itself. She swirled and sipped, chatting all the time about the charms and delights of the wine. It was not a technical tasting, but a sensual one. She talked about romance and exploration, carrying us to the distant corners of the world with her spices and experiences. And her final comment topped off the presentation like a cherry on a sundae. "This wine," she sighed, "is like drinking cashmere."

The other speakers had all received a nice round of applause for their efforts. But only Leslie received an audible moan of pleasure before the applause. Because she had reached the audience on a different level; she had done more than educate them, she had touched them.

That was great marketing.

Of course, there are many men who will read this and disagree. They will point out that the people they talk to are buying their wines, and the system they are using is working.

Is it?

On that same wine conference trip, I had dinner at the café in a hotel near the airport, full of travelers waiting for the next flight. A group of three men sat at the bar, drinking a beer, watching a ballgame, and generally hoping that somehow they would avoid being bored for the evening. And they were bored.

As I ate my dinner and watched, a group of four young women approached the bar. They were obviously interested in having a drink, but a little concerned that the men might pester them. What happened?

The men each took a shot at trying to make them laugh—but each was clearly far more interested in impressing his friends than actually talking to the women. The women stood clear of the bar, quietly discussing their options. And then, just as quietly, they turned around and walked out of the bar.

The men then congratulated each other on their witty repartee, laughing all the while.

But I was looking at the bartender. He stood there helpless, as his potential customers chose to go somewhere else. What did it cost him? Ten or fifteen dollars in tips? And it cost the bar another fifty dollars in drinks? Why didn't he offer a solution? Why didn't he offer to let the women sit at a table far from the bar, or in another part of the lobby? He was young, he was inexperienced, and I don't think he really understood the situation. And so he returned to serving another round of drinks to the three men at the bar.

Which reminds me of the wine industry...

When it comes to wine, many men think they are experts, and they well may be right. But that doesn't mean they know how to convince women to buy their wines. Wine consumers are women, and I am not sure women want to be convinced, so much as charmed. I think that they would like to be invited to participate, instead of being treated as students who need to be educated. I think that they would prefer that the conversation focus around their interests, instead of the wine industry's interests. When it comes to wine, I think most women would just say,

"Honey, we have to talk."

CHAPTER 13

SAMPLES AND DONATIONS—AND HOW TO USE THEM EFFECTIVELY TO BUILD YOUR BRAND

Samples are one of the most valuable assets at any artisan producer, but they are often sent to the wrong places, at the wrong time, and for the wrong reasons.

There are some pretty simple solutions to how to approach the subject, but most of us are so deeply into the swamp that we don't have time to think strategically. So instead of a strategic plan, what we use is a shoot-from-the-hip plan. And we measure the results accordingly, if we measure them at all.

If you've read this far, you know that I am a huge believer in developing budgets, goals, and expectations. I like having measurable costs, verifiable activities, and quantifiable results. Let's take a look at how that plays out when it comes to product samples.

What's the Point?

First of all, let's decide why we are giving product away for free. In my mind, there are really only two reasons. Either you have a great product and you want to make sure that everyone knows about it, even those who might not pay for it, or you have a lot of product that isn't selling, and you would really like to make sure people have a chance to taste it, even those who might not buy it.

While on the face of it these two scenarios are similar situations, the ways they play out in a marketing plan are very different. Let's take a look at both scenarios to fully understand how they work for a mix of audiences, from media to trade and consumers.

In each case, let's keep in mind the two primary forces in marketing: push and pull.

Push is when you exert your marketing and promotion force to encourage the distribution network to hurry the product along the pipeline. The goal is to gain distribution, placements, and visibility on the shelf.

Pull is when you spend your marketing and promotional dollars to generate demand on the consumer end of the pipeline. The goal here is to create such demand that the product is sucked through the pipeline.

Of course, the perfect marketing strategy will use a certain amount of each, so that the push and pull help each other out, and the flow through the pipeline is increased noticeably.

How do samples accomplish these goals?

With the Media

Samples can generate both push and pull. A strong recommendation from a writer will not only grab the attention of the consumer, and drive them to a retailer to purchase the product. It will also grab the attention of a retailer, restaurateur, or distributor and encourage them to give you more visibility...pushing it forward into the face of the consumer. By providing samples to one key writer, you can influence a wide range of your audiences. That's why they pay PR agencies the big bucks!

How should you approach media samples?

If you already have a relationship, the strategy is straightforward. If you have met the writer, and established a solid reputation for the product, then a sample mailing of new releases is absolutely in order. Make sure the writer has everything he or she needs to write the story, including background on the product, the company, and retail prices.

A trifold brochure

Because you already have a relationship with this writer, you should already know what kinds of products he or she likes, and have a rough idea of how he/she will respond to these new samples. Use that information to carefully select both products and writers so that your media sample budget does the most good.

Those are the easy ones.

If you are just starting out, or if you are dealing with a writer you've never met, then you simply have to do your homework. Begin by reading the columns, and understanding what products and styles are most likely to get positive attention. Look for story angles that tie into the passion and knowledge of the writer.

Then look at your product portfolio. I am usually opposed to sending out the complete series of new releases to a writer. I prefer to pick one or two things, my best foot forward, to begin a relationship between a writer and a company. In the perfect world, that new IPA we are releasing is exactly what the writer is most interested in covering. It's more likely that the product we do best may not be what the writer likes best.

Don't force the issue. Remember that these relationships are for a long time, not just one article. You are better off waiting until you have something that will really appeal to the writer than sending off something that will send the wrong message. You never get a second chance to make a first impression, and the first product you send should send a very clear message: This is a company that bears watching in the future.

On a more general note, writers are always interested in what is new and what is trendy. Writers have to follow the trends to stay current, and if your products can help illustrate what is good about the trend, you are in the perfect spot to get some great media attention. Package these samples with background information appropriate to the trend: sales data, national demographic data, or even news stories from the general media.

Another approach is to package your products with others from a region or a category that gives the writer all that is needed for a serious article about the whole subject. These samples will almost always get great attention, because they provide both educational content and market context. If you wonder why your own samples aren't getting tasted, you might ask whether they are providing those same elements to the writers.

But there are two additional factors that play a role in this decision. The first one is that the lead times for most publications are many months—by the time the sample is sent, the product is received, catalogued, and tasted, the article is written, and the magazine is published, you may already be sold out!

With the Trade

Sometimes I think that the oldest trick in the book is the comparative tasting. At one point or another, every salesperson from Robert Mondavi to Laura Chenel has said, "Take your best, and taste it against mine!"

Somehow, you have to get out of the middle of the pack, and the easiest way to get their attention is to put your product up against their favorite. They don't have time to talk or listen, but in the right situation, such a tasting can open the door to new accounts and major new markets.

It would be nice if the trade always tasted like this in a direct comparison tasting, but it is much more likely that you are going to find yourself in a room filled with other companies, all competing for the attention of a beleaguered target market of buyers. It will do you no good to complain about the rules; this is the way the game is played in many markets. Instead of complaining, learn to take this situation, grab it by the throat, and play to win.

Here are a few basic rules that will give you an even chance:

Stand in front of the booth, not behind it. Key contacts are always in demand at a trade tasting. Have an assistant behind the table, so that you can stand in front of the table, pursue key contacts, and spend some time with them as they walk away.

Always have a little something extra under the table. This is a sure way to get a little more attention, and will give you one more reason to spend extra time with the people you really need to talk to.

For Consumers

Most of us get invited to participate in so many tastings that if we accepted them all, we would never have to sell a thing—we would have given it all away.

But that isn't exactly the goal, is it?

Which leads to the obvious question, what is the goal? If you don't know, then go directly to jail, do not pass go, and do NOT collect $200. Every one of your free samples should have a specific goal attached to it. Write it down and keep it in mind. And track the results for every tasting and promotion. At the end of the year, this is the single easiest way to decide which events and tastings get your support, and which do not.

For consumers, you still have to answer the basic strategic question: Do you lead with your best foot forward, or push what you really need to sell? It is very tough to take a product that is on allocation and give it away to consumers. At the same time, if your top competitors are serving something great, then you should seriously consider matching their efforts—or run the risk of ending up in second, third, or even last place.

One caveat that I must raise is the confusion that often arises around an enthusiastic employee pushing a specific product that doesn't sell well off the shelf. DO NOT, under any circumstances, draw the conclusion that this is a good product that just needs a little help. If you are making something that doesn't sell without a free sample and a sales pitch, you are not making a product that will sell in the general market. Save it for your tasting room, where you can give it that attention.

What Happens Next

Whatever use you choose for your samples, please remember that providing samples is only a small part of the project. You will simply not get your money's worth if you don't develop and execute a comprehensive follow-up campaign to cement the relationships that the samples have begun.

Think of a sample as a first date. What follows is ever so much more important! In this case, the new social media, combined with a good old-fashioned telephone, will make a huge difference. When we can, we try to use company principals for media follow-up, because it does such a good job of building those relationships for the future. With the trade or consumers, the follow-up should be done by those who are really hoping to benefit from the relationship, and are in a position to close the sale.

If you do it right, you will never think of samples as something that you have given away for free; they will be investments in the future that pay great dividends in both the short and the long term.

And then there are the donation requests.

Every artisan producer has the same problem. Once you announce that you are going to handcraft a delicious product from locally available ingredients, you will start getting the invitations to provide some of your precious product to a local charity. For free.

That's only the beginning. Some of us receive as many as one hundred requests for donations every week. Most, if not all of them, are from very worthwhile organizations who are working hard to make our country and our community better. In fact, it would be pretty darn easy to give away the entire annual production just to support these charities.

Of course, most of us take a rather reactive approach. Each letter requesting a donation is reviewed and judged on the merits of the organization and the potential benefits the donation might generate. Then the decision is made, and either the product is donated and delivered, or the request is denied.

Sample of Tour de Cure's regional sponsors page from its promo materials

The challenge to all of this, of course, comes at the end of the year. How do you judge the effectiveness of your donation budget? How do you measure the results you have achieved? And how do you justify the expenditures for these donations, when you can't really measure the results they achieve?

So what are the answers?

First of all, you already know some of the answers. While all of these organizations are doing good works, not all are appropriate to your business. A donation of wine to an organization that is dedicated to the reinstatement of Prohibition is just not in the cards—unless you are really looking for the wrong kind of publicity.

Other organizations are simply too far away. While you might well consider making a small donation to help raise funds for a library in your community, you would probably not support the same efforts to buy books for a library in Bulgaria. At least, I hope would you wouldn't.

But those are the easy ones. And what every company really struggles with are the hard ones.

The real solution to the issue of donations begins at the very beginning, when you take a reactive approach. Because a good donations program should begin not with letters from charity organizations, but with your marketing and communications plans.

Doesn't it always?

Begin by defining your category and positioning in that category. That should go a long way toward helping you determine what kinds of events and organizations you want to cultivate. The first level of selection should be the demographics of the organization. This assumes that you know the demographics of your target market well enough to judge.

The classic matches for artisan producers? Find people with similar interests and passions: wine, fine art, classical music, food and wine societies, public radio and television, and the like. The only problem here is that everyone else also wants to appeal to these same audiences. And one of the basic rules of marketing is that you should try to be the leader in everything that you do. It's a big pond out there, and most artisan producers are pretty small fish. We have to find our own pond, most of the time.

Of course, this gives rise to the classic marketing question: Should you be where everyone else is, or should you strike out on your own to find new audiences? The question is a complicated one, but for most product donations, I am not a big fan of being one of a hundred producers in a crowd of people who don't know what they are eating or drinking or why. I would prefer to find my own group, build a long-term relationship, and have a few close friends that are exclusively mine.

Then I would work hard to make that group into missionaries for my products.

You can ask for exclusivity with an organization, and hope that this will give you the leadership position you want. But bear in mind that such positions are valuable enough that other companies might well outbid you for the next year. If you do a great job of taking advantage of the opportunities presented by an exclusive sponsorship, your efforts are often rewarded by increased competition for this spot in the future. Plan for that, and make sure that you won't have to reinvest every year in a new relationship.

The relationship is really the key. You should be looking for organizations that want a long-term relationship, one that is equally beneficial to both parties. If you provide all of the money and product, and you don't receive good value in return, then you are wasting more than your product and money; you are also wasting your time. And your competition is gaining on you.

The ideal partner for a donation program would be an organization with demographics that correlate very closely to artisan foods, and that can offer a wide range of opportunities and media to help you build rewarding relationships with their members.

- A newsletter that goes out to all their members is a great place to tell the story of your company, position your products, create some brand awareness, and encourage trial. See if you can explore the various opportunities in a newsletter with the organization. Can you suggest recipes using your products? Can you have a regular column in the newsletter to talk about your interest in the organization? Can you get a feature story on your donation in the newsletter? Those are real, measurable goals—goals that will help you get ahead of the competition.
- If the organization does exclusive membership events, can you provide product for these events in return for some higher visibility? Charity organizations are always happy to receive free products—but you still want to negotiate that price. In the best case scenario, you would be the title sponsor of the event, would have signage that clearly showed your support, and would have something for each member to take home that reiterated your name and the reason that you have so much in common with the members. You would be invited to provide a speaker at the event, who can tell the story of the company and its relationship to the members and the organization's cause.

- As publicity for the event unfolds, you should ask that your name be positioned prominently in all releases and information. While it is true that this "shared attention" can take away from the primary goal of the organization, you should be able to negotiate some kind of solution that will make you both happy.
- Your website and the charity organization's website should have links and share content to explain your relationship and why it is important.
- The media are another example of shared attention. While you would love to be featured in stories about the charity organization and its work, you should also explore with journalists in your world who share the interests and concerns of your selected organization. You may well find that your support has built a much stronger bond with a key writer—one that you can explore further with other elements of your PR campaigns.
- In return, you might offer to give the organization more visibility by creating POS (Point of Sale materials) about the organization for your retail displays. This gives them great visibility with a new audience, gives new customers a reason to try your product, and gives your existing customers another reason to buy your product. That's the kind of attention that most charities would deeply appreciate—and it doesn't cost much, either.
- If you have a newsletter, it is the ideal medium to promote this relationship to your customers, and achieve those goals as well.

Having said all that, there are some additional concerns you simply have to address. We frequently find that our target consumers have little in common with some of our other key audiences. While our dedicated consumers might well love the idea of an exclusive reception at a modern art museum, it is pretty hard to use that same reception as an incentive for the distributor sales force. We have developed some wonderful partnerships over the years with organizations that were perfectly positioned for the target consumer—only to find that the additional tickets we gave to the sales force were tossed away or, in one memorable case, scalped on the front steps of the museum by one of the distributor salespeople's girlfriend.

Another issue is the interest in building relationships with organizations well outside the normal arena of food and culture. Artisan producers throughout the world have experimented with a wide range of activities and organizations, all seeking to find that unique niche that will give them direct and rewarding access to the perfect combination of consumers.

NASCAR, sailboat races, the PGA, Major League Baseball, rock and roll concerts, and all sorts of other events have been tried. In most cases, they have not been wildly successful, often because those attending the events are not primarily fans of artisan products—and support for these kinds of organizations ultimately fall into that wonderful no-man's land of Lord Leverhume. You remember him, don't you? He said that he knew half of the money he spent on advertising was wasted; he just didn't know which half. This is usually true when you support events that don't have a traditional link to your kind of high-end food products. You know that SOME of the audience is interested, but it may well be that the rest of the audience is not even slightly interested...and that can distract from the overall image you create at the event.

Some of the very best matches are ultimately so expensive that they simply cannot make any financial sense. It would be wonderful to be the official sponsor of the Olympics, or to underwrite the National Football League, but that kind of money simply doesn't exist in our industry. The fashion industry, while not quite in that category, combines many of the classic demographic matches with some high end food products. But it is also a very expensive game to play. If you want to have your products at the top design shows, you will not only need to pay a pretty penny for the privilege; you will also have to spent a good deal more to create the kind of image and positioning at these events that will gain the attention and admiration. It isn't enough to stand next to the star; you will have to get them to smile, shake your hand, and act as if they are happy you are there. How will you look, standing next to Claudia Schiffer? Don't worry—the good news is that nobody will notice!

And we can never forget the local charities that really do need our support. Whatever national marketing goals you may have, I suggest that every one of us has a responsibility to the local community that cannot be ignored. There is a basic element of goodwill that cannot be earned any other way. You should give to local charities, and you should do so for commercial reasons as well as for social responsibility. And if you really want to make a difference, give more than product. Give the time and energy of one of your employees for a few hours a month. This will not only help the organization, but it will build the very thing that makes the world go 'round—good relationships with key audiences.

In the end, your donation budget needs to be as carefully considered as any campaign you manage, and it should undergo the same rigorous cost/benefit analysis that you use for all of your marketing communications. You and your team should agree on the goals of the program, the strategy and tactics to be used, and the results you expect to see. You should all agree that the results you expect to generate are well worth the dollars they will cost to achieve. If they are not, why would you choose to spend the money this way?

If you do this right, donations can become a key factor in your marketing and sales success. Your donations budget can play a key role in developing positions and image for the company, increase sales, and add visibility in the media. Or you can sit at your desk, and hope that the right letter happens to drop in your lap.

Now let's talk about getting free exposure on television and the movies.

One thing we all want is visibility. Where you are seen, and with whom, can really make a difference in how the market perceives your product. In fact, the whole concept of product placement is based on an old adage: You will be known by the friends you keep.

Product placement is a simple process: Working behind the scenes, you get your product in movies, TV shows, and other sorts of high visibility locations. When James Bond specified Dom Perignon in the movies, a whole generation of Bond wannabees found their new luxury brand, even if Bond usually drank other champagnes in the original books by Ian Fleming. That was great product placement. The figure I have been quoted on that placement was $100,000, which seems really cheap in retrospect.

But the value of product placement is wildly controversial, and much of the value has to do with more than just visibility. It's a complicated game, and it's easy to be fooled into thinking that it is much more valuable than it is. There is nothing worse than getting to the end of a big product placement campaign and seeing that sales figures are still flat, that consumer awareness hasn't improved, and that lots of dollars have been spent.

Over the years, I've been involved in some major product placement programs with my clients. In almost every case, we got great placements in some of the best and hottest shows on television. But after a couple years of this kind of success, we still had a very hard time documenting the impact this had on brand awareness and sales figures. In the end, most of our clients have moved on to more measurable and results-oriented kinds of campaigns.

What Impact?

Many product placement services or companies simply try to get the product on the show, or in the photo shoot. While this does give you some visibility, I don't think that it creates enough positive buzz for the brand to be worth much money.

Over the years of working in this business, I spent a lot of time trying to make this work, and trying to figure out why it doesn't get the kinds of bang that we wanted for our buck. It took my fourteen-year-old daughter to show me where the shortcomings of product placement lie.

One night at home, I walked through the family room while she and a friend were watching one of their favorite TV shows. And sure enough, right in front of my eyes, I saw one of my agency's top brands in the hand of one of the show's big stars.

"Hey," I yelled. "That wine is from one of our clients! That's a bottle of our wine he's holding."

My daughter was quick to react. "Dad," she said. "Be quiet! We can't hear what Ross is saying to Rachel!"

Exactly. While we can talk all we want about subliminal advertising, the truth is that merely showing a bottle on a television show doesn't make much of a difference in the marketplace. The people who are watching the show may love the Pottery Barn look of the set, but that doesn't mean that they are actively trying to identify the specific sofa in the scene. In fact, most of our labels are not striking enough to be identifiable at thirty feet away. The result is that the only people who really notice are the people who make our product—and we are NOT a target market.

Is it really worth the costs of most product placement campaigns just to see your cheese in the hands of a television star…knowing that the audience itself is unable to identify the brand? That brand identification depends, of course, on two completely unrelated elements. The first is your own package. Dom Perignon has a very easily identifiable package, so showing the bottle may actually have an impact, but most of us don't have that kind of packaging. One label looks enough like another that consumers can't really be counted on to make a positive ID.

The other factor is equally important. If the audience watching the show isn't really paying attention to the wine brand, then it won't identify your brand even if it COULD tell which one it was. If the most important thing on the show is the expression on Rachel's face, then it is too much to expect for viewers to tune into the fact that it is your product in Ross's hand. Our products are props, not the star of the show, and there isn't a show in the world that would change that.

And even better example of this was an effort a few years ago to get a Jeroboam of Perrier-Jouët Fleur into the Victoria's Secret catalog. The effort was successful, and sure enough, there was a full-page photo of the gorgeous Heidi Klum in a negligee, holding the beautiful bottle.

Did I mention that Heidi Klum was in a ravishing negligee? I did. She was. And the bottle didn't get nearly the attention we hoped. Most people were far more interested in the model and what she was wearing than what bottle happened to be in her arms.

So why do companies do this kind of thing? Sometimes it is simply a question of making the owners feel good about seeing their product in these kinds of situations. One of the worst kinds of PR is the kind that makes the agency and client feel really good without having any effect at all on the marketplace. That is my fear with a lot of the product placement opportunities we face.

It really doesn't matter how *you* feel about these programs. What matters is how *the market* feels. And unless there are some very special circumstances, it is extremely hard to measure how the market feels. If you can't measure the results, then how do you know that you are doing any good at all?

The answer is you don't. You don't know at all. And I don't like to spend money that way, whether it is mine or my client's.

What Does Work?

Like the James Bond placement for Dom Perignon, there are product placements that really have made a difference for the future of a product.

In the best of all scenarios, product placement goes far beyond a brief shot of your product in a television show. If you can actually be lucky or rich enough to get a star on a show or in a film to specify your brand by name, then you can expect to get a fair amount of attention from that. That's great product placement, and it is worth lots of money.

It's just really hard to make it happen. Given that there are so many other industries that have so much more money to throw at this sort of thing, smaller artisan producers usually get the short end of the stick. When compared to the fashion industry or major brands of distilled spirits, our budgets simply aren't in the same league. That makes it hard to get the best placements. We usually have to settle for a short shot here and there, with predictably minimal results in the marketplace.

It certainly makes sense to make the most of your fame, once you get noticed. Make sure that you document every appearance, by capturing a screen shot, taking a photo, or even chasing down a video clip. These can't become press releases—no journalist will write about the fact that some other journalist wrote about you—but they can be valuable resources for your website, social media efforts, or sales presentations.

One of our clients was very successful at donating product to television shows. It seemed as if his products were being used by every character in every sitcom in Hollywood. That didn't boost his sales much, because the people watching the show were much more concerned about the jokes and the situations than they were about noticing product placements. But he then made a video reel that he showed at all his sales presentations. The salespeople were excited to see his products get that kind of attention and exposure, and he often got a standing ovation.

Similarly, if one of your products appears in a Pottery Barn catalog, or Williams-Sonoma, that has a positive impact on your brand. But be careful about reproducing that kind of artwork. Most of it is copyrighted by the catalog publisher, and they will have some concerns about you reproducing it outside of their control.

Yes, even on your website.

One simple option for local producers is to make your products available for use in shop windows in your community. If you showcase your products on Main Street, that will attract attention from both consumers and trade customers, and if you pick the right shops, it will also help position your products in just the right light—literally.

This isn't revolutionary. Major brands in America compete to be in shop windows on Fifth Avenue in New York City. You are just aiming for the low hanging fruit that lives just down the street from your offices.

The other thing that major brands do is to incorporate celebrity spokespeople to promote their products. You probably can't get Meryl Streep, but even asking your local neighbors and friends to speak up for their love of your products will generate additional awareness and recognition. And some of them may turn out to have quite a following in your neck of the woods.

We worked with one small bank that featured a few of its customers in local advertisements in the town newspaper. While they are not sure it increased their customer base, they reported that many of their other customers came forward to say that they wanted to be featured in similar ads, and the customers they did feature reported increases in both attention and sales. That's a story they could use for years to come.

CHAPTER 14

CRISIS PR—WHAT TO DO WHEN THE SHIT HITS THE FAN

Every year the media is full of stories about product liability and consumer complaint issues, from accelerating Toyotas to exploding airbags. While it may be somewhat reassuring to think that we don't have many of these kinds of stories in the world of artisan food and drink, the truth is that they happen all the time. They may not be as dramatic as an exploding Pinto, but almost every company has had some sort of problem along these lines, from scuffed labels to a batch gone bad. We certainly have seen a lot of companies fall far short of their revenue and profit projections, or go out of business. That's not the kind of news that helps any of us.

As public relations professionals, we are usually judged by how often we get our clients and products mentioned in the press. But in many of these cases, the true test of our ability is just the opposite: Have we limited the damage that these situations can create for the brand? Some of my best work will never see the light of day, and I am delighted about that. The story could have been blown out of proportion by a news-hungry press, and we were able to avoid that.

Let's take a look at these situations to see how they can be handled in a way that is best both for short-term results and long-term goals.

What Exactly Is Your Problem?

The first step in any crisis management situation is to clearly and completely define the problem. This is often much more complicated than you might first expect. Sure, your production team may be doing the kind of QC monitoring that recognizes and identifies any and every problem. But the chances are that the first time you learn of a problem, it will come from one of your customers, not from your team. At that point, it is crucial that you really dig into the problem and get all the facts.

Here is where it gets a bit tricky. Facts aren't all what they seem to be, and we should never forget that marketing is a battle of perceptions, not facts. So while your production team may suggest that the problem is limited to a certain product, bottling date, or label run, it's a good idea to include a lot of other people in this exploratory stage. I've found that tasting room employees are frequently more aware of these kinds of issues than production department employees, mainly because on a daily and monthly basis they open and taste more product that anyone else. And they get to see the reactions of the people who see and taste that product.

But don't just limit your questions to the production team and the tasting room manager. If you have a distributor, retailer or restaurateur who can be consulted in complete confidence, it's a good idea to do this as well. We've all heard about companies that have come to love a particular flaw in their product, and it's always a good idea to get an honest outside opinion on the matter. I don't believe that I have ever worked on a consumer complaint/product liability problem without discovering that there were many different versions of the situation. If you have a consultant, or local technical laboratory, that would be another obvious avenue to getting real answers about what is going on in and outside the bottle or product.

Finally, a legal point of view is critical to understanding some of the issues involved in product liability and consumer relations. You overlook this at your own peril.

At this point I like to get everyone in the same room and ask for a complete debriefing of everything we know about the situation. I work really hard to make sure that we are not convincing ourselves of something that won't stand the scrutiny of a serious inquiry or investigation. This is the time to ask the hard questions, suggest the unthinkable possibilities, and really make sure that everyone in the room is clear on what happened, why it happened, and what kinds of impacts it is going to have on product perception, product quality, product safety, and product liability. This is ground zero, and you have to make sure you really get to the bottom of things.

Be very careful about how you do this, because once you make these decisions, going backwards will not only be very difficult, but will also call into question every part of the company, its management, and its relationships with its customers. Get it right the first time, even if it means that you have to run a few extra tests, or take another day or two to get the full answer.

How Could This Happen?

When you discover the full extent of the problem, you will also have developed some theories about how it happened, and why. These may play a big role in determining your actions moving forward, but I would suggest a major caveat here. Your product may not taste good because, for example, the packaging you received was flawed, but in the eyes of your consumers that does not automatically absolve you of all blame. Pointing fingers at this point may not actually improve your image over the long haul. Others in the field may well suggest that you have a responsibility to perform proper quality control on your vendors.

In the end, no matter who else was involved in this situation, your company produced the product in question, and released it to the public. In the eyes of your customers, it is your responsibility to make sure that the product meets their expectations. If you failed in that, it is of little importance to them that others may have been involved. It's your name on the label, and it's your problem to solve.

That's a good perspective to carry through all elements of this process, by the way. No matter what factors were involved, if it is your product, it is your problem. And it's the future of your brand that's at stake.

Of course, a huge factor in your decision-making at this point is going to be the size and seriousness of the problem. The spectrum is enormous, and the range of responses is almost as large.

How Bad Is it?

One end of the scale is that your artisan creation is potentially dangerous to the health of one of your customers. In that case, there is no question of the appropriate response. You must immediately recall any and all affected products, and spare no expense or effort in reaching out with a warning. There will be no sympathy or understanding for a company that allows its customers to get ill simply because they are trying to pretend there is no problem. But if you are taking all due precautions, that scenario should be relatively rare.

What is more likely is a defect or problem that affects the product's flavor or appearance, but does not create any health concern at all. Then the obvious question that must be addressed is a simple one: Is it bad enough for someone to notice?

There is no easy answer to this one.

One of the most common wine consumer complaints is the existence of tartrate crystals in the wine. Any enologist will tell you that these are not, in any way, dangerous, nor do they affect the flavor of the wine. But some consumers see them differently—even mis-identifying them as shards of broken glass. What should your response be?

Over the years, my company has done what you should do today: develop a series of standard responses to these kinds of consumer complaints. In each case we explain the background of the situation, and why it is not a cause for concern. But in every case we also offer some kind of a solution to consumer satisfaction. For all the good explanations in the world, an unhappy consumer will not buy your product again. And we view every interaction with a consumer as an opportunity to build a long-term relationship.

Some problems, such as those created by bad storage conditions, may have been caused by the consumer himself/herself, or have happened as a result of poor shipping or storage conditions through the distribution system. Once again, while these are not technically your fault, the end result is the same: the product doesn't taste as it should. It is up to you to suggest the solution that satisfies its customers.

And some products will show no flaw at all. How should you respond to a customer who simply doesn't like what you have put into the package?

Answer that question, and you have a good start on dealing with the rest of the issues that can arise in these situations.

Now What Do We Do?

Some companies have a very straightforward customer satisfaction policy: If a customer is dissatisfied with the product, the company will be happy to replace it. Period. Given the low rate of consumer complaints that usually arrive at most companies, this policy is one that makes a lot of sense.

But then there comes a day when you notice that you are receiving more than the usual number of complaints, and they all seem to focus on a single aspect of the product. At that point, it is time to draw the team together and figure out what is going on.

It's important to remember that in many cases, you will not see a lot of the problem product. It will, instead, be found in the back rooms of restaurants waiting for a visit from your distributor. Or they may be found half-full, in the trash can (or recycling bin) of a retail customer. These are the ones that really hurt—because you don't know about them, and you can't resolve the problem. You can only kiss that customer goodbye.

You begin to wonder if maybe your distributors are beginning to notice a pattern here. And your club sales dip just a little bit. Or your retailers no longer order ten cases of product, but only three. In these competitive times, you can't afford those kinds of results. And it is one thing to offer to replace a single package, or even a single case, from a dissatisfied consumer. It's something else entirely to have to think about hundreds or even thousands of boxes that are falling short of your image and hopes for the brand.

It is always tempting to think that if you just don't say anything, the problem will slowly and quietly go away. Nobody will notice, and in a few months, you'll have transitioned into your next production run, and will be able to sleep again at night. There is some merit in that suggestion; if the flaw in the product or the packaging is very slight, it just may work. But if the flaw is just large enough that someone really does notice, and starts communicating with other people about it, then the problem can get a lot bigger in a hurry. Social media can get this situation out of your control almost overnight.

In the old days, the fear was that a newspaper or television show might suddenly start to investigate the story—and bring ruin upon the brand. But these days, all it takes is a few consumers who are willing to post something on Yelp! or one of the other social media sites, and your brand name is in play in a very targeted media. It doesn't take long for the word to get out!

One of the great truths in human nature is that once someone starts to talk about something like this, just about everyone starts to notice it. And then what was a very minor flaw, in your mind, becomes a steady current of critical communication about your brand. If that happens, expect a lot of those people to be asking a very pertinent question: If you knew about this, why didn't you say anything or do anything about it? Perhaps it would have been better to deal more openly and directly with this issue. While it may send an immediate message of concern to the customer, it also sends a message that you share their concern, and value their goodwill.

Many companies choose a middle path, deciding that they won't actually mention the issue, lest they draw attention to it. But they also have clear guidelines for everyone at the company on how to respond to any customer who might bring forward a concern or a complaint. That approach, particularly when the offer to replace the product or reimburse the customer is given quickly, freely, and openly, can be a very good plan for companies facing this kind of issue on a limited basis.

But do not forget your most important customers—those in the sales and distribution pipeline. It is crucial that you do a good job of reaching out to the distribution pipeline in a situation like this, and offer both support and effective solutions. By providing your distribution partners with the information and actions they need, you can often earn their trust and appreciation. That will come in very handy in the years ahead, as competition for their attention becomes even more intense.

Problems like these create enormous stress, but they also offer a company a chance to show exactly how committed it is to living up to the promise of its brand. In the long run, that is the real secret to success.

But What If They're Wrong?

There's that old public relations adage: I don't care what you say about me, just make sure you spell my name right!

That's not really a good philosophy in terms of marketing communications. When we spend many months and mounds of money to develop a key communications campaign to support our brand, we want the media to get it right.

Now I know this won't come as a huge shock to you, but the media isn't infallible. Over the past few years we've seen all sorts of examples of how the media get things wrong, from guessing wrong on election results, to falling for quite elaborate hoaxes, and everything in between. You can find a number of these errors in any daily newspaper. As any newspaper junkie will tell you, Page Two is where you find all the corrections to previous editions.

The only saving grace to this situation is the sheer volume of stories that the media cover every day. Given that immense figure, it's not surprising that they get a few things wrong. It's far more surprising that they don't make mistakes more often. But that is small consolation when the mistake concerns your brand, your company, or your clients.

The real question is, what can you do about it? The answers to that question are more complex than you might imagine.

Let's begin with the one that most people get wrong:

Does It Really Matter? Why?

I know. You've spent a ton of effort to get the story written and published, and then you see that one of the products is misspelled. Instead of Sauvignon Blanc, the article has it as Sauvngon (sic) Blanc. Is that worth calling up the writer, so that you can point out the error of his ways?

Not in my opinion. Chances are that it is a typo. Chances are that someone else will bring it to his attention. And even if they don't, virtually all the readers will know what he meant anyway. Now if the article had spelled it Sauvignon Bland, there might be more reason to complain...unless the writer intentionally spelled it that way.

That's another problem entirely.

What are appropriate reasons to call a journalist and correct a story? Some obvious examples are when the name or title of a company employee is incorrect, or dates are wrong. If the story suggests that you are primarily a dry cider producer, and yet seventy percent of your production is sweet wine, that would be worth mentioning to the writer. You can provide hard facts to support your correction.

I've seen way too many owners get offended by something that is a really minor matter. Unless it is damaging to your brand or company, let it go. If you make a stink about it, the journalist may well correct it. But the next story may be a long time coming, as the journalist decides to work with less picky individuals in the future.

The thing to remember here is that journalists really DO want to get it right. They hate being wrong, because their job is to get the facts, and share them with their readers. If they get something wrong, you'll find journalists will bend over backwards to correct that as soon as possible, because it's important to them, too. But only if it is really important, and only if they really are incorrect.

They will not be very receptive to a request to "change a quote in the story" if your spokesperson said something stupid and now wishes he hadn't. A quote is a quote, and if someone from your company said it and it really captures what the journalist wanted to hear, then you are going to have a hard time getting that changed. If the quote cites inaccurate information, you might get that clarified. But if you simply stuck your foot in your mouth, you probably won't be allowed to pull it back out again. After all, journalists are just like everyone else, and we all think that a Freudian slip is deeply revealing, even if it isn't what the speaker meant to say!

Make Sure You Have Your Facts Straight

Of course, you are perfectly within your rights to request a correction on any fact in a published article that is wrong. They key word here is not "perfectly" or "rights"—it's "fact." If a journalist decides to phrase something differently than you did in the press release, don't automatically assume that he is going to want to change that when you ask him to do so.

This is a really nebulous area, and you need to proceed with caution here. Phrasing and innuendo are not facts, and a journalist is usually completely uninterested in changing a story just because you would have said it differently. They don't like admitting that they made "mistakes" based on the "fact" that you would have phrased it differently. If they got the gist of the story correct, they're going to let it stand as is, and they are going to defend their position vigorously.

Many journalists these days will avoid addressing a difficult question head-on. Instead of taking sides on the issue, they will quote you on one side, and quote or paraphrase your opponents on the other side. You can't correct what your opponents are quoted as saying. It's an attributed quote. It's their opinion. And they are entitled to it, as the journalist is entitled to quote it.

And don't confuse facts with opinions. Way too many people in our business confuse facts with opinions, and then want the media to correct those.

If one publication gives your product a rave review, and another publication hated it, those are opinions. You can't call up one of them and insist that they change their article based on what the product REALLY tastes like. They tasted it. They didn't like it. And no phone call from you about what somebody else thinks or wrote will change their mind. Don't waste your breath or their time.

On the other hand, some writers sometimes do give products a second chance, particularly if you can explain why the product they tasted might not have been at its best. But be prepared for the results, because if the product tastes the same to them the second time around, you might not only get a second note—you might also have convinced the writer that you really don't know what you are doing. That's not good. Which brings us to the next point.

Make Sure You Really Want to Talk About It

If you want to argue a point with a journalist, remember that the writer will really want to make sure you're not just "spinning" the story to your own benefit. That means you are going to get a much more careful and critical interview about the subject.

If you don't like the fact that the journalist mentioned his or her perception that there is an elevated level of a certain chemical in your product, from salt to alcohol to lead, be prepared for a fight. What will you do if the journalist asks you to submit the products to an independent lab, so that you can both work with the same data? Will those lab tests show that you have been absolutely accurate? Or will they show a discrepancy? You can be assured that the writer will mention that in any follow-up story. And your efforts to correct things will have backfired completely.

Once you bring up a topic with a journalist, it is fair game. If you have any skeletons in your closet, they will come out. If you have someone in your company who might have a different version of events, you may see that information in print. And if you want to make an even larger issue of it, remember who will have the last word. It won't be you.

Remember Tommy Lasorda's quote? "Never argue with people who buy ink by the gallon." They own the story, and they get to decide who will have the last word. It will be them. After all, they have a professional interest in being right. When it's time to call a journalist and ask for a correction, keep that in mind, and stick to the facts.

Be Quick About It

In the bad old days of print journalism, you might ask for a correction in the next edition. It would get printed on Page Two, and it would be there for all to see. Today, with the immediate changes available on the internet, you can get the story changed within minutes of when it appears, if you've done your homework right.

(And yes, I know that lots of people don't read Page Two. I can almost guarantee that the size of the story with your correction will be much smaller than the original story that got it wrong. Partly that's because your story is no longer news—it's old news, and the media doesn't make money publicizing old news. But it's also because your correction shows that they were wrong, and while they are willing to admit that, they sure don't want to put it on the front page. That's reality, and you have to accept it.)

But the flip side of this coin is dangerous. In these days of internet access, an incorrect story can go viral very quickly, either through email distribution lists or through any variety of social media. The sooner you contact the journalist and correct the story, the fewer people will have seen the original and erroneous version. And the fewer people might cut and paste the story into something they are writing, multiplying the error.

Don't Forget To Say Thanks

I can't remember the last time I called in a factual correction to a journalist and wasn't thanked in return. A good journalist always appreciates the help, particularly if I wasn't part of the reason that he got it wrong. Once the media gets a chance to verify my correction, they are more than happy to get it into print as soon as they can. After all, they don't want to go down in history as the people who got it wrong.

And I am always both gracious and helpful when it comes to these kinds of conversations. I know how hard it is to get things right. In my business, we send a memo out after every meeting, summarizing the meeting and the decisions made. Why? Because so often people have differing memories about what happened. If that happens between colleagues who work together regularly, it shouldn't surprise us that it happens with writers who are covering a story or industry that's new to them.

In the end, we both just want to get it right. And that's the way we should both approach it.

CHAPTER 15

PLANNING AND EVALUATION

Evaluating the results to make sense of it all. From the old clip service technology to modern Google word...and how to create an evaluation matrix that will make you more effective by focusing on message, market and publication/audience.

Public relations is challenging. It seems that no matter how carefully you plan things, there will always be something that gets in the way of your perfect plan. As the old adage says, "There's many a slip twixt the cup and the lip."

That doesn't mean you shouldn't plan. In fact, we much prefer to plan out our Public Relations programs as much as a year in advance. We do this for three reasons:

1. It allows us to make sure that everyone is on board with the plan, so that we don't spend a lot of time later in the year thinking through the basic concepts. That happens right up front, and we address all the big questions at the beginning.

2. It helps us answer that age-old question of everyone in the PR business: "What are you guys doing?" We don't have to answer that question; we can simply point to the plan and say, "Check the workplan, look at the calendar, and you'll know exactly what we are doing."

3. It allows us to plan out our time effectively. In every PR plan, there are times of intense activity, and times that are slower.

When we know in advance, we can plan to use that downtime to start prepping materials or clearing the decks so that crunch time doesn't mean disaster time.

If you want to plan your public relations activities for the next year, where you do start? That part's easy. There are some basic elements to any public relations program that can be identified well in advance. Set those up first, because they will give the plan some structure, and then add in the other activities where and when they make sense. It helps to start with one big calendar, either on-line or on paper.

If you think of public relations in its simplest form, you often think of working with the media to get your message out to your various audiences or publics. And if there is one thing that we can guarantee about the media as a whole, it is that it is unpredictable at best. While there are any number of "regular" stories in the media, from Veterans' Day to New Year's Eve, the biggest stories of the year are always a surprise. After all, that's why they call it the news!

(Of course, in this book I have suggested that public relations goes far beyond working with just the media, but the long term goal is still the same. And the unpredictability is also the same.)

That doesn't mean you shouldn't have a plan. We love clients who work with us to develop a long range plan for the year. That plan gives us everything we need to do good work for the client for the next twelve months, and both we and the client have agreed on what we are going to try to achieve. That makes the work a lot more rewarding.

As I mentioned in Chapter Two, some of our clients in the European Union receive grants or other types of support, and this kind of a plan is a critical part of the funding process. (These types of grants are also available in the U.S. from the USDA or state government programs that support small businesses.) The government officials want to know what they are going to get, and they want that information to be as specific as possible. Since we've worked with some of these groups for many, many years, we're very comfortable with the process and the terminology.

So what goes into a good year-long public relations plan? We start with the basics: Positioning and key messages. If you don't have these, you simply can't do good marketing or public relations. You need to define who you are in terms of your competition, and you need to do it in a way that is easy for your customers to understand and repeat. If you don't know your messaging, there is no reason to contact anyone else. You have nothing to say. A good public relations plan will have this messaging right at the top. That will help you work with graphic designers as well, since they need this information to capture your messaging in graphics.

Audiences and key markets: Unless you are a massive national brand that hopes to be all things to all people, you will have to refine your plan so that it focuses on those markets that are most important to you. And you won't be reading this book. A good plan will identify those markets that need extra support to grow, as well as those markets that are so important that they must get attention to keep the sales flowing. And your audience goals should also clarify the roles that the on-premise and off-premise channels play in your business. Smaller companies will want a tight geographic focus, so that they don't waste money trying to reach people who are not in a position to become customers. For every audience, you should have messaging and a plan, and you should have a list of audiences for your plan. Don't forget your own employees, local authorities and regulatory agencies, and the people who can make your life miserable...like your neighbors!

Expected developments: Every company should have a projection for sales activities that includes new product releases, new label introductions, and the like. These projections form the building blocks of an annual plan. You need to send samples of products out to the media when they are first released, not when they have been in market for ten months. That's not news. So your public relations plan should include all of these dates, with supporting activities. This is also where you need to list any plans for future expansion into new markets, and how you are going to support those with public relations efforts.

Enter these dates as blackouts: between Thanksgiving and New Year's Day, and Harvest. You should eliminate the first dates because nobody in their right mind wants to deal with PR people during the holidays—not the trade, not the media, and not the winery spokesperson. And while the harvest is a great time to meet with the media, host events at the winery, and generally take advantage of the excitement around the vintage, most winemakers don't have a spare second during this time.

Once you have all of these basics in line, we can start to work on the delivery systems. You will want to map out when you will use press releases or media pitches to get the key messages to those audiences. The new label story should be sent to your entire distribution network, along with any marketing materials you have developed to support it. New products need new fact sheets updated on the website, and new vintages do as well. All of this can be charted out well in advance, so that you should never find yourself selling into the marketplace without the appropriate POS support materials.

If you sell outside your local area, you need to include a section of the plan that addresses when your top management will travel to those markets to support the brand. Try to plan this out in advance, to the point of identifying key writers you may want to meet during the visit. Major media writers often book their schedules months in advance, so it is important to check these dates with the writers and make sure that they are open.

You should also be able to identify special events that you have selected to reach particular groups or audiences. I've already written about how important these events are, and how important it is to have measurable goals and objectives for them. Write it all out as part of your plan, so that you can always know (and SHOW!) how you are doing.

If you have the money to organize your own events on-site or in other locations, these should also be included in the public relations plan and calendar.

When you are done with this calendar it should contain the following:

>> Enter the release dates for all the new product releases planned for the next year. Once you have those dates, count back two or three months. That's when you need to enter the development of the fact sheets, the new release letter, and the list of media that is going to receive samples. It all needs to be done, and it needs to be done BEFORE the product is released and shipped to the media. If you have a fan club, you'll also need to include those materials in this effort as well.

>> Enter the dates for any proposed market travel. About two months before those dates, you'll need to start contacting media

to see if they have time to meet with your spokesperson. By then you'll need to know what your pitch is going to be, and you'll need to have your materials developed as well. So add those on to the calendar where they belong.

>> Enter the dates for all the major consumer and trade events that you will attend. It will be much harder to set up media visits around these events, since lots of other people will be in town at the same time. But you need to get these on the calendar so that you can understand where your spokesperson is at all times. Obviously, you can't plan to host events or media if your host isn't home.

>> Enter the deadlines for all the major competitions that you are going to enter this year. Count back at least two weeks to give yourself time to track down all the information needed on the forms, get the entry fee checks written, and the samples all packed up and shipped out.

>> Enter the editorial calendar dates from every one of your target publications, so that you can track when they are going to write about products that you make. That will give you time to submit samples and perhaps chat to the appropriate writer before the story goes to press…rather than after it has appeared!

>> Enter the dates for any major charity events or projects that you have planned for the next year. Count back two or three months to make sure that you have time to develop the PR materials, contact local media, and get your local or regional salespeople involved in the event.

>> And every company needs friends. Sure, you have a few, but you can always use more, can't you? Part of making friends is finding strategic alliances with partners who share your goals and interests, but don't compete for your customers. It is not always possible to lay out the complete strategic alliance at the beginning of the year, but you should have a few options in the plan. If you have some of these in place, then you must have a clear idea of what you expect them to do for you. Write it out and track it.

What's That, You Say?

How will you track it? How will we know that it is working?

I thought you'd never ask.

As I mentioned in Chapter Two, this is a key part to any public relations plan. You must develop metrics for all these activities, and they should be included in the plan. You might consider focusing on the media for one part of the plan. You will want to generate stories in key publications, and you will want those stories to emphasize the key messages of your brand. If your campaign generates a story that includes those key messages, that's a solid win. Congratulations. Now go work to get some more.

This is where the European Union model falls apart a little bit. What I've written here sounds like a recipe for a great public relations plan, doesn't it? It is. But as you work your way through the year, you will find that some of these elements are really going gangbusters, and others.... not so much. Maybe they can be fixed, but maybe they are simply not going to work this year, with this product for this audience.

Good football coaches often start the game with a list of some fifteen plays that they think might be successful at the start of the game. These are things they believe will work, and if they do work, the coach will continue to pound away with them.

But inherent in that game plan is the possibility that some of those plays might not work, or that some of the plays will turn out to be unstoppable. This is where the European contract system breaks down; their contracts are set in stone, and don't allow much flexibility at all. When something works well, we don't really have the resources to move ahead more aggressively with it. And when something seems less productive, we can't stop doing it to focus on more rewarding activities. We simply have to fulfill the letter of the law.

Which brings us to what you should be doing with your public relations plans. I hope you started with a well-thought-out plan that addresses all of the goals and objectives you have for the year. And I hope that you included a system of measurements that help you evaluate what is working and what is not.

At least twice a year, you should be looking at that plan and measuring the results, and making the changes you need to make to win the game. That's what good coaches do. That's what winning coaches do.

One of my staff members once came into my office to ask a simple question: "How much is it worth to get a client on a local TV station?"

Of course, she and I both knew that this was not a simple equation, and as we set about trying to develop an answer based on data and facts, we also had to overlay a matrix that concerned what the client, herself, perceived as value. The exercise took my staff member several hours to compute, but still only reached a rough approximation for an answer.

An explanation of the process she followed is a good way to begin a discussion about this topic, and how both agencies and clients can approach the answers.

One of the biggest questions in public relations has to do with the value of the press coverage generated by the campaigns we organize. The factors involved are really quite complex. On the one hand, we have the more or less measurable factors: circulation, cost per thousand for the publication's advertising space, number of times the story is reprinted, etc.

Circulation is the number of readers who will see the story—and those figures are a regular part of any publication's marketing efforts. You can almost always find them as part of the advertising sales package they present. On-line publications are harder to evaluate this way, as is social media. But you can certainly track the number of followers on any Twitter account, or the number of friends for every Facebook page.

If it would cost $5,000 to take out a full-page ad in a local magazine, isn't a full-page story about your company equally valuable in that same magazine? It's the same space, the same publication and the same readers. But it's not always the same impact. So here's how to do a better job of evaluating the public relations coverage that you generate.

Let's look at the softer data, which is equally important. Does the story do a good job of really capturing the message of the brand, or does it actually present information that is contrary to that message? Is it a feature story, or a simple list of artisan companies from a given region or participating in a given program? Is the story in a publication that the brand manager has highlighted as critical to their success, or is it in an unrelated magazine that most of her market will never see?

Years ago we worked with one of our favorite clients to develop a system that allowed us to do a much better job of tracking the results we were generating in the media. And you can apply these same criteria to the coverage you generate with your donations, special events, and other promotional activities.

We began with that basic tool of the public relations industry, the clip report. You can hire a firm to track all the stories that appear about your company or your brand, or you can track these same stories via Google or another key search engine. One way or the other, you'd like to get a handle on as many of these articles as possible, and you'd like a way to catalog and categorize them later.

We start with collecting those stories and entering the circulation numbers for each story. Now it's time to start thinking.

How will you catalog them? The system we developed used three key elements to rate any story that appears:

>> Does the story do a good job of communicating your key brand message? It's one thing to get a story about you and your family in the local paper, but if most of the story is about the church that you attend, rather than the bread you bake, it won't do you much good in the long run. The stories that do a good job of promoting your key message get their circulation numbers multiplied by a factor of two, because they are at least twice as valuable.

>> Is the story in a publication that reaches one of your key markets? Same rules apply here. If the primary goal of your PR campaign is to drive customers to visit your bakery in Louisville, a story in a magazine in Seattle won't do you much good. But a feature story in the local newspaper will have a big impact. Here again, these stories get their circulation numbers multiplied by a factor of two.

>> For those of us in the more focused gourmet world of artisan food and beverage, the publication itself makes a huge difference. While we'd love a story to appear in the food section of the *New York Times*, or a top gourmet magazine, a story in *Fast Food World* isn't going to do us much good. With this in mind, we ask our clients to identify the key publications they really want to notice them. And when we get an article

placed in one of those publications, we multiply the circulation numbers by a factor of two there as well.

All this multiplication may seem a bit disingenuous at first. After all, if we compare the size of an article in a publication with what it would cost for the same size advertisement, how can we justify claiming that the article is so much more valuable than the ad?

It's simple, and it points to one of the key advantages of public relations over advertising. Advertising is you talking about yourself, and it's not nearly so credible as when an objective and independent expert conveys your story effectively to a target market. You may think that you make the best IPA in the world, and you can say that as much as you want. But when the *Washington Post* writes an article about you and says that you make the best IPA in the world, believe me, it makes a difference!

What do you do with all these stories? Many companies are so excited about getting some good news in print or on-line that they fail to take full advantage of these stories until it is far too late. The time to strike is when the iron is hot—to borrow a phrase that harkens back to a time long before the internet.

When you get a good story, share it with the world. Put it on your website—with a link on the homepage. Format it so that it's easy to copy, easy to forward and easy to link, and send it out to your entire sales network, from distributors to local accounts. Share the link with your consumer fans on social media, and invite them to visit and share in the celebration with a special price on a key product.

In short, get that story out to everyone you can possibly list as a friend or family member, with one exception. Do NOT send that story to other journalists or contacts in the media. If you do, you will be telling them that they don't have to write a story; it's already been written. Even worse, they might think that you are telling them that they should write a story JUST LIKE THIS ONE. You can imagine how much a writer likes getting that message.

But once you have distributed this story far and wide within twenty-four hours of when it appeared, your work is not finished. You should have a list of great stories about your company on your website, and you should add this one to the list. You should also make that list available to anyone who is selling your products, so that they can show it to potential customers and win you friends. Once a good story has appeared, it should become part of your on-going messaging about who you are, and whether or not you should be taken seriously in this very competitive business.

Chapter 16

Lies, Rumors and Getting Your Priorities Straight

Five Myths

Over the past couple of years, I have been contacted by any number of people with suggestions for topics of presentation I might make, or articles I might write. It is great fun, and has led to some very interesting and amusing conversations.

Many of these people are simply responding to the situation of the moment. They are furious that their client or owner doesn't really understand the issue from a Public Relations point of view. If only I could write an article about it, then all would be clear.

Well, thank you very much. Some of the ideas are quite good. But given that this is a book with a firm deadline, I'm working a bit ahead of the curve here. If you are going to have an argument about these topics in a management session two years from now, please let me know about it ASAP, and I will be happy to weigh in with a chapter in the next edition of this book that outlines your position effectively.

On the other hand, some of the suggested topics are classics. And many of them seem to come up often enough to fall under that category of Great Myths. These are commonly repeated truths about Public Relations that everyone knows—and every one of them is false. Let's look at them one by one.

Myth #1: "It Doesn't Matter What They Say, As Long As they Spell Your Name Right"

This is an easy one to refute, if you know how. Whenever a client mentions this approach to me, I have an immediate response that seems to slow the discussion down to a manageable level.

If you would like to see your name in the paper, walk down Fifth Avenue in New York stark naked. Explain that you are doing this to promote your concept of pure, unadulterated products, and you are going to do this in every city in America. The strategy is flawless, but few company owners will accept the challenge.

(If you ever meet one that does, please refer him or her to me. I can get a lot of mileage out of that story!)

So it does matter what they say. In fact, it matters a lot.

A few years ago, I took a call from a journalist who was doing a story on a major wine trade organization. The journalist had reached the conclusion that the trade organization was not serving all of its members equally. He was looking for a winery spokesperson who would be willing to say that in some very quotable language.

"Just give me someone who will say that it is all a waste of time and money," he insisted. "I've got the rest of the story written; I just need that quote!" He was very unhappy when I told him that none of my clients wished to go on the record with that kind of language. I explained to him that my clients had nothing to gain from making such a comment, and that it could damage their relationships with some of their colleagues.

Which is a good question to ask yourself every time you get a call from the media. To really understand strategic Public Relations, you need to run every media request through a simple analysis:

- Is my participation in this story going to negatively affect my relationship with any key audience?

If the answer is yes, then think carefully. Remember Br'er Fox: he lay low.

But sometimes the request can lead in an unexpected direction. Many years ago there was a grape grower convicted of switching grape varieties when delivering the harvest to a few wineries. They thought that they were buying Chardonnay, but were being delivered Colombard instead. When a well-known *San Francisco Chronicle* reporter called to investigate, I recommended that my client not respond.

Another winery owner did respond, and found himself quoted in the paper as saying that he couldn't really tell the difference between the grapes that made fifteen-dollar-a-bottle wine, and those that made five-dollar-a-bottle wine. The writer had a field day with that quote.

The truth to the myth: If you can get one of your key communications points into the story, and not alienate a key audience, then go for it. Otherwise, when you are tempted to say something really, really controversial, don't.

Myth #2: "Media Contacts Are The Secret to Great PR"

This one is a classic. The implication is that journalists are silly little sheep, without a brain in their tiny little heads, just waiting for their good friend the Public Relations professional to fill their minds with good stories and bad ones.

I have a lot of friends in the media. We often talk about our professional interests in food, wine, beer, olive oil, etc. But that doesn't mean that I can tell them what to write. It doesn't even mean that I can always suggest what they write, or how they write about it. It does mean that they usually return my phone calls, when they are not on deadline.

And if I have a good idea, they will listen to it. But if their editor has a different idea, or they think the story should go in a different direction, they will tell me. Just as any friend would tell another.

True, we share stories and perspectives. But I know many journalists who have told me that they no longer write about this company, or no longer really want to talk to that PR person, because they felt pressured to always write about them.

I have pitched many, many stories over the years to journalists I have never met, or even talked to before. I pitched those stories not on the basis of our non-existent friendship, but on the basis of the quality of the information I could provide. Sometimes those journalists so appreciated the information that they called me when they had other questions about the world of artisan food and drink. Were we friends? No. But we did develop a solid working relationship.

Journalists have their own jobs to do. They take that role very seriously. They like PR people who understand that, and work within the rules. Sometimes those relationships can also grow into friendships. But it is the rare friendship that can overcome the natural concern for journalistic integrity. And it is a rare journalist who can afford to put journalistic integrity on the line for a friend in the business.

Frankly, that's a good way for a journalist to lose a job.

When I interview new employees, I am always interested in the media they list as good contacts. I am not interested because I think somehow that we will be able to shove a story down that writer's throat; that's simply counterproductive. But I am interested in talking to that writer. I am interested in knowing how this potential employee works with the media. Does he/she establish credibility and trust? Is he/she responsive to requests? Is this a person the journalist sees as a valuable contact, or just a nice friend?

Those valuable contacts will get the job, every time. They will get the job because they know how to work with the media—whether they are best friends or not.

Myth #3: "Creativity Is The Secret to Great PR"

We all know a story about a clever Public Relations professional who created great coverage for a client with a stroke of genius. It happens. But in my conversations with the media, one of the most commonly used phrases is "PR Gimmick." And it is not used in a complimentary way.

What's the explanation?

What strikes one writer as clever (and witty!) may well strike another as a complete waste of his time and energy.

I remember a well-known writer who once wrote an open letter to Public Relations people who served him. He extolled the virtues of creativity and humor. He waxed poetic about some of the clever and fun campaigns that he had received. He snorted at those who took a more conservative approach. He pleaded with us to have fun, be creative and be silly.

When I discussed the column with another writer, the response was emphatic. "Please don't waste my time with that crap," she said. "I am a journalist. I have deadlines to meet, and stories to cover. If you have real information that you think is important, get it to me. If you don't, please don't waste my time with stupid gimmicks."

As Public Relations professionals, our job is to make both of these people happy. And there is only one way to make both of them happy: We need to develop a different approach for each writer.

A journalist who doesn't usually write about food might well be interested in a basic story about how olive oil is made, or how a wine and food pairing is done. But someone who has covered the industry for years needs something else entirely.

When you have a great story to pitch, then this becomes fun. You can take the basic information of the story, and craft it in different ways to pitch it to different media. An overlay of one kind might work for a trade journal, while another approach might work better for a lifestyle magazine. This is one of the real challenges and real joys of working with the media.

And it is hard to do when the goal is a mass mailing to a wide range of writers who might be interested. We try to keep these to a minimum, for obvious reasons. We also often try to walk a delicate line, providing just a touch of creativity in our mailings, without obscuring the main point of information. We like to get their attention with something clever, but then the meat of the story has to be crystal clear.

After all, if the main point is lost among all the creative hoopla, then you really need to go back and read Myth #1 again.

Myth #4: "Build A Better Mousetrap, And The World Will Beat a Path to Your Door"

This is simply not true, and it is the basis of so many marketing campaigns that it has done real damage. This is the philosophy of the production-driven company: that the product is the only thing that matters.

If you believe this, you really should start reading the business section of the newspaper from time to time. Wall Street is full of stories of companies with great products that failed in the market.

It is particularly ironic that this should be true in our world, where we sell products that are judged on subjective, not objective standards. These is no such thing as a perfect food or wine (except, of course, yours!). What one expert considers to be lovely, another can judge as too ripe, too green, too spicy, too coarse or too earthy. In our world, there is no such thing as a demonstrably better mousetrap.

The perception of your company in the marketplace is a combination of the classic four "Ps" of marketing: Product, Price, Promotion, and Placement. Ignore this at your peril.

It is also true of Public Relations programs. If you create a better story, you have only done half the work. The other half of the work is to get out into the market and tell that story to your key audiences. If you don't have a plan to do this, you really don't have a plan at all.

All too often, your story sits quietly in your computer, or on a website, while your competitors are out in the marketplace, telling their own story with conviction and personality. Their story may not be as good as yours, but their delivery system is a lot better. And in the end, what is communicated is not what is said, but what is heard.

The market is not hearing your story. And they are not looking for a better mousetrap.

Myth #5: "We Have a Great Story"

Sadly, this is usually not true. Movie producers and authors often complain that everyone they know has tried to sell them their life story, because it is so interesting. And even with all of these unsolicited stories, Hollywood still struggles to put good stories on the screen!

The truth is that most of us do not have riveting stories. Yes, the owners might be interesting people. Yes, they make good products. Yes, the fact that they support the arts is laudable. Yes, they should be congratulated that their products were served at the White House, won a Gold Medal, or received a rave review from a publication. Yes, it is interesting that the owner made money in another business before she dedicated herself to perfecting balsamic vinegar. Yes, it is interesting that he or she has always had a passion for...whatever.

But in the end, none of this adds up to a story. And none of it is unique.

A great story, from a Public Relations perspective, is one that will capture the imagination of everyone who hears it, and that will capture the essence of what you are all about. It should be unique. None of the elements mentioned above are unique.

To be truly unique, you have to take chances. You have to make products that others avoid. You have to make decisions that fly in the face of the accepted wisdom of the industry. You have to go boldly where no one has ever gone before.

There are few of these in our business. And so the Public Relations efforts of the rest of us have to get down to the simple hard work of doing what everyone else is doing—doing it harder, better, and more effectively.

Yes, you will need to use your media contacts and your creativity. You will have to act as if your product really is a better mousetrap. You will have to do whatever it takes to get your client in the newspaper, and make sure they spell the name right. If you do all of that, it just might be a really good story.

How Much Does All This Matter?

After all, since your beer tastes better than anyone else's, why should you even care about this book?

Over the years, I have spoken at more than eighty industry, trade and consumer conferences. I love meeting the many owners and employees who attend these conferences, and I enjoy the give-and-take conversations that take place at them.

But one thing has always amused me about these conferences. They generally have two seminar tracks. One is for the people who make the product, the production track to address all the technical elements of baking, making, pressing, fermenting or finishing the product.

The other track is for marketing and sales. For most small companies, that means that one person attends the production track, and the other person (the sales/marketing/PR person) attends the marketing track, where I am speaking.

The seminars are always fun and educational, but I always find myself thinking, "The wrong people are in this seminar. The people who really need to hear this presentation are next door, learning about the technical aspects of production." Because so often, these artisan companies begin as hobbies, and unless they are directly tied to a business plan that includes developing a successful marketing and sales plan that sells their product at a profit, they will never become real businesses.

Success in our industry isn't just about making good products. Forget that old saying that if you build a better mousetrap, people will beat a path to your door. First of all, nobody is looking for a better mousetrap. And secondly, our world is full of subjective products where terms like "better" and "best" are rarely used with much effect.

Making a good product isn't the solution to your marketing and communications problems; it's the basic entry fee to be in the business at all. If the product you are making is not good, you should close your doors. But don't make the mistake of thinking that making a good product will solve all your problems. That's where PR and marketing come in.

What does success mean in our world? Success isn't making good products. Success is making products and selling them at a good profit. That means that you should spend as much time thinking about how you are going to sell your products at a profit as you do thinking about how you make it.

What's the solution? Time, focus, and energy. It's that simple. Marketing and communications are highly valued skills, and should be learned and respected. You should focus on them just as intently. And in the end, it all comes down to one key message: You should tell a good story.

What's Your Story?

What is a good story?

On a trip to Italy last year, I was invited by one of my hosts to visit a small country inn in nearby Slovenia. The day was drizzling with rain, and the small country roads that wandered through the Slovenian hills seemed to take us both far away and back in time. The rain washed all detail out of the landscape. We didn't get lost, but we did have to stop a few times to look carefully at the road signs, and then consult our map. When we arrived, we weren't sure we were there.

The building was from hundreds of years ago, like the rest of the buildings in the tiny town, and only a small sign on the massive wall identified the inn. We ducked under our umbrellas and raced through the old wooden doors into the inner courtyard, which reeked of horses and cows that were stabled nearby. Here the rain had puddled up in places, and the cobblestones were slick. We carefully worked our way across the courtyard to the door of the restaurant, where we could see the warm light of a fire and candles glowing through small windows in the thick walls.

And here is where it gets really interesting. This small inn still makes and cures its own meats and sausages. Dinner was simply a selection of these cold cuts, served with baskets of homemade bread and carafes of the local wine, both red and white.

My host was enthusiastic about the food. We had to try every variation and variety of the cured meats, and I have to say that his enthusiasm was absolutely deserved. They were stunningly good, and astonishingly flavorful. Platter after platter, and board after board came out of the kitchen, often with a sharp knife to help us slice up the offering.

The bread was rich and heavy, with the kind of texture one no longer sees in the modern world. The flour was coarse, and it gave both weight and flavor to the bread. It was the perfect complement to the rustic meats.

And the wine? My host was embarrassed. "You are an expert. You drink great wines from all over the world," he said. "I am sorry these are so bad." As an enologist, he could not bring himself to enjoy the wines. He finally ordered himself a beer and one for me as well.

But I was enchanted. The wines were served in earthenware pitchers, and drunk from heavy glass tumblers. The white wine was thin, acidic, tart, and green, with a hint of volatile acidity. It would have immediately been eliminated from consideration at any serious wine competition. And the red? It was equally rustic, with the same tart character and a healthy dose of green tannins. Neither of these two wines could be sold in the U.S. market. Served in crystal goblets in my home in Napa, they would have been poured out into the potted plants by my guests.

But I was enchanted because I was not really drinking wine—I was drinking history. I was travelling in time. We had left our car outside the heavy walls of this country inn, and were now living in another century— hundreds of years ago. From the fireplace to the tiny windows, the room was unchanged, I was sure. The food was exactly the same as it was five hundred or a thousand years ago. And so was the wine. It was a meal I will remember for the rest of my life, because it took me to a place and time I had never been before. I will remember the winery and the wine- maker as well. He took me outside his winery, to give me an experience to remember—one that he shared with me. That's great marketing.

For many consumers, our products are more than just something to eat or drink. They are tickets to an adventure, an invitation to explore. When a consumer buys our product they want to take a trip to a different time and a different place, where people are still in touch with the earth and their sense of time has slowed to match that of Mother Nature's.

How do you make that trip a reality? Please don't talk about the end- less details of your production methods. Don't sell based on chemical analysis or production technology. That isn't what we want to hear.

Tell us a story. Take us on a trip to a different place, and let us fall in love with it. Tell us what about your destination is truly unique and wonderful.

And if you can get any of those sausages, please let me know!

CPSIA information can be obtained
at www.ICGtesting.com
Printed in the USA
LVHW021250040920
665076LV00017B/881